D0903959

All the Best,

Edward Share

# *Patches of the Quilt*

Tiger Iron Press
Macon, Georgia, USA

# *Patches of the Quilt*

## True Stories From a Children's Home

Written by

**The Adults They Became**

Edited by

**Edwin Chase**
**Bill Chase**

**Tiger Iron Press**

http://www.TigerIronPress.com

*About the cover:* In every age there are children who must confront the harsh realities of a world that seems devoid of color. But here and there and now and again, the breath of God's spirit brings new life, hope and vibrancy to an otherwise drab, despairing landscape. The girl stands frozen yet captivated by the beauty of the quilt that seems to dance in the breeze, symbolizing the warmth, nurture and comfort that all children long for. The quilt pictured is called a "home quilt," and is meant to be used every day, making it a perfect symbol for the Methodist Home.

Cover design created by artist Julianne Gleaton.

Printed in the United States of America.

ISBN-10: 0-9787263-3-2
ISBN-13: 978-0-9787263-3-1

Search by: children's home, history of orphanages, Methodist Home for Children and Youth, child welfare, Georgia history, South Georgia Conference, family counseling

First Edition: September 2008

## *In Memory of Jesse Boring*

A Civil War chaplain who guided the Methodist Church to acquire the property that became the Methodist Home.

## *In Honor of Frank Jones*

A distinguished member of the Board of Trustees whose law firm has represented the Methodist Home for more than a century. Frank Jones' father and grandfather both served as Chairmen of the Board, and his great-grandfather wrote the Methodist Home's By-Laws in 1872.

# *Table of Contents*

Introduction                                                    ix

Chapter 1:  Whose Children Are These?                            1

Chapter 2:  Boys Becoming Men in World War II                   47

Chapter 3:  Never a Dull Moment on the Farm                     69

Chapter 4:  When Having Fun is the Main Event                   89

Chapter 5:  Stellar Mischievous Pranks                         103

Chapter 6:  The Wonder and Excitement
                    of Saint  Simons Island                    115

Chapter 7:  Reflections on a Childhood Restored                131

Chapter 8:  Rock and Roll on the Back Porch
                    and Monopoly on the Front                  153

Chapter 9:  The Patches Continue in Wondrous Patterns          185

About the Authors                                              207

Acknowledgements                                               215

Afterword                                                      217

# *Introduction*

In the stories that follow you are invited to see the world through the eyes of a child beholding the ocean for the first time, or a precocious girl enjoying the pleasures of summer, or the wonders of a starry night. You are invited to walk in the shoes of a platoon leader directing his troops into battle for the first time. You may marvel at the lengths some boys will go to play a prank on some unsuspecting soul. You may be surprised to find God in the most unlikely places. It's all here.

*Patches of the Quilt* is a collection of true stories written by the men and women who grew up at the Methodist Home for Children and Youth in Macon, Georgia. These stories began to surface at Homecomings. Whenever former residents got together, they shared old times. And over the years those stories have been honed and now have attained a richness and texture that is palpable.

The stories joyfully recounted here serve as a boundary against forgetfulness – lest they slowly fade with the passing of time. There is something sacred about the stories of our lives because they define who we are as individuals and shape the way we see our families (in this case, the Methodist Home).

The title, *Patches of the Quilt*, was derived from a welcoming ritual that began in the early 1980s. Since that time, whenever a child arrives at the Home, he or she is given a new, handmade quilt, and is told, "Like this quilt, you are unique and worthy to be cared for. We will do our best to care for you. You do your best to care for yourself." The beauty and softness of a quilt, the talisman of warmth and comfort, are remembered long after the words are forgotten. The quilt with its array of patches emerged as a perfect metaphor for the Home.

The "patches" representing the Methodist Home are infinite in number and include every aspect of the Home: the more than 10,000 children who have been given a new lease on life since 1872:

the churches of the South Georgia Conference
members of the Board of Trustees,
the professional staff,
foster-parents,
volunteers,
and donors.

Because this book is historical in nature spanning more than a hundred years, it is chronological in spirit with the oldest stories in the earlier chapters and the more recent ones appearing later. Every chapter is preceded by an introduction that sets the tone or the historical background for the stories.

Our hope is that these stories will connect with the story line of your life and strengthen your faith in the goodness of God.

# *Patches of the Quilt*

# Chapter One

# *Whose Children Are These?*

When Jesse Boring, a Methodist Chaplain, saw the large number of orphans who slept in the streets and alleys following the Civil War, his first question was, "Whose children are these?"

He immediately responded, "Our children," and under his leadership the Methodist Church acquired a small orphanage located in Macon, Georgia.

In 1887 when the main dormitory at the Methodist Home burned leaving 50 children homeless, the question was raised again, "Whose children are these?"

The Vineville Methodist Church responded, "Our children!" And the members of this congregation opened their hearts *and* their homes and provided a place to live for these children until the dormitory was rebuilt.

From the turn of the century until 1940, our nation confronted World War I, the worst influenza epidemic to strike America and a debilitating depression. Whenever children were displaced in the midst of these traumatic events, the question was asked again, "Whose children are these?" And congregations across South Georgia responded with enthusiasm, "Our children!"

The waning years of the Nineteenth Century and the early years of the Twentieth provide the setting for the stories included in this chapter. They provide a rare glimpse into the events, hopes,

1

and dreams of a generation that Tom Brokaw referred to as "The Greatest Generation."

Courtesy of the Middle Georgia Archives, Washington Memorial Library, Macon, GA, circa 1894

**Main Building of the Children's Home, Built in the 1890s**

## *The Painful Price for Barnyard Fun*

### William Kirby Smith, Sr.

The Home operated a dairy and vegetable farm that provided food, milk, and butter for the residents. At age six my first job was in the dairy turning the cream separator. An older boy, Eugene Klein, loved to play tricks on Mr. Dillard, the Farm Supervisor. One day while six or seven of us boys were in the barn, Eugene said we all would get a great big laugh when he wired the dairy barn door to the electric current. Mr. Dillard got quite a *shock* when he opened the door. Well, there was no surprise when the Super ordered all of us to form a line and bend over the cow trough. With a two-inch leather strap he warmed the seat of our pants!

When the other boys and I were a little older – but not yet teenagers – our chores included cleaning the barnyard. Now, that was some job! Imagine assigning that chore to a young boy today with this order: "Collect and place all the dried cow manure pies in one large pile!"

We did that chore but not without some fun. There were two bulls, one a big Jersey and the other a big black and white

Circa 1946

**The huge barn, hayloft and silo were perfect places to pull pranks.**

Holstein, that were in adjoining pens with only a gate between them. We knew if these feisty bulls got together, they'd have one heck of a fight! So, led by Eugene, we decided to open the gate and let them at it. The only trouble was we didn't know how to separate them once they commenced fighting. When Superintendent Dillard came and saw the bulls fighting and our laughing, it was back to the cow trough and his leather strap. For some of us, learning was a slow and painful process.

We had our fun, no doubt about it; but early on I learned the value of hard work and the importance of accepting responsibility for my actions. I have always been thankful for my early training at the Methodist Home.

# *The Girl from Mississippi*

### Ida Ruth Sheffield Sanders (daughter)
### for
### Ida Tamsy Brooks Sheffield

My mother, Ida Tamsy Brooks, was born in Mississippi in 1874. When her father died, her mother brought her to Georgia to live with relatives. When her mother died, Ida's relatives brought her to the Methodist Children's Home in Macon. She was about eight years old.

While living at the Home, she became a well-rounded child. The older children assisted with the needed work at the Home, which included caring for the younger children. One of my mother's jobs was to make biscuits for breakfast. She spoke of making 60 to 80 biscuits each morning.

My mother was fortunate in that she was taught cooking, sewing, and piano. She was one of those fabulous cooks who never used a recipe. She was also an excellent seamstress who could look at a garment, cut a pattern, and duplicate almost anything she saw.

She loved to tell of the few times when it snowed in Macon. The children at the Home would get bowls and gather snow, sprinkle sugar and vanilla on it, and eat it like ice cream!

Her talent at the piano and organ led her to Miller County when she was eighteen years old and ready to leave the Home. She taught music and married my father, James Sheffield. They had six children, five girls and one boy. I am the sole surviving child. I am grateful for the opportunity to relate some details of my mother's early life. We have all been enriched and blessed by her love and talents. Most of the members of our family are Methodists, and I feel certain that this fact is a direct result of my mother's years at the Home.

# *My First Day at the Home*

## James Kent

It all started the night before I arrived at the Home. My brother, my sisters and I were told we would be leaving the family we were living with for another home. We were also told we would never be coming back. The fact that we were leaving the family we had come to like and were comfortable with was very upsetting to the four of us. We let the world know it by crying and otherwise causing trouble. Then the real bombshell hit.

A strange couple arrived and informed us that they were there to take our baby sister home with them. They made it very clear that Anne was to become their daughter. Also, we were told we would never see her again as she was to become their little girl and assume their name. Georgia, Wiley and I did everything possible to prevent this from happening. We even tried physical force, but three kids less than ten years of age were not very forceful. After the three of us were soundly spanked for this disruption, our baby sister was escorted out the door. We did not see her again for 32 years.

The next morning we and our meager belongings were loaded into a car. It was the first time that I can remember riding in a car. The trip seemed to take forever. Other than the length of time, the only thing I recall about this was going over a very high railroad trestle. I just could not believe that man could build something that high. I was really frightened.

At last we arrived at the Home. We stopped in front of the office which was in the same building the Home uses as an office today. I believe it was Mr. Daugherty who met us. As we disembarked from the car, I heard loud squeals coming from the basement of the office building. It sounded to me as if several children were being punished at the same time. The squeals made me think that the discipline had to be severe. I panicked, and dived back into the car!

As I recall, Mr. Daugherty called his son to the car and asked him to take me to the basement so I could see for myself the source of the squeals. After much persuasion, I accompanied him to the basement and learned that the squealing sounds were coming from a pen of guinea pigs. I was very much relieved.

We were upset to learn that we would be placed in separate cottages, but things quickly quieted down after being assured that we would see each other several times a day, especially at mealtimes. Also, it was pointed out that we would not be that far apart because the cottages were fairly close in proximity.

Courtesy of the Middle Georgia Archives, Washington Memorial Library, Macon, GA, circa 1953

**As the sun went down James Kent's first day at the Home concluded with a series of pleasant surprises.**
**(This photo represents the evening meals in earlier years.)**

The next big event of that first day took place at suppertime. This was our first meal at the Home. My sister and I were seated at a table with five other children and an adult. I sat in wonder, as I had not seen so much food on a table at one time, if ever. Supper was served family style and each one had a large glass of milk by his or her plate. The glasses caused a problem for us. They were tall glasses filled to the brim. The adult began passing the bowls of food around, and we served ourselves. I received the first bowl, helped myself and tried to pass the bowl to my sister. I did not lift the bowl high enough and over went the glass, spilling milk everywhere! I held my breath. To my surprise, there was no fuss and no punishment. Just a fresh glass of milk! Then my sister knocked over her glass. The same thing followed: The mess was cleaned up and a fresh glass of milk appeared.

**A Fresh Glass of Milk**

Seeing this, I began to feel relaxed for the first time. I knew I had found a good place or more accurately, a good place had found me.

# The Ringing of the Chapel Bell

## Alexander A. Scarborough

In the 1930s, the ringing of the Chapel bell at 5:00 A.M. set that summer day's typical routine in motion. The pigs were fed with shelled corn kernels and leftover garbage food hauled in a big barrel mounted between two large wheels and fronted by a long extended handle pulled by two boys. The 19 cows were fed hay and milked. The milk was filtered and hauled in five-gallon cans to the kitchen where it was put through a cooling system. Part of it was churned to make butter, which always went well with the fresh biscuits at breakfast time. This 12-hour feeding/milking cycle, always initiated by a ringing of the Chapel bell, would be repeated at five o'clock in the afternoon, seven days of the week. Breakfast, signaled by another ringing of the bell, was finished before beginning other farm chores.

The tomatoes were picked in the early morning before the heat of the sun drove away the morning dew. This was the time a freshly picked tomato from the underside of the bush tasted its best. The bright red tomatoes were carried in a tall bushel basket to the kitchen to be prepared for use in the midday meal in the newly renovated McIntosh dining room beneath the Chapel. Fresh corn on the cob, corn bread, and prickly okra, cut with care, rounded out a delicious meal. The summer heat demanded two or three glasses of iced tea to quench a thirst well earned.

The summer weather was too hot and humid to sleep comfortably for the required one-hour after-lunch nap. Because electric fans were in short supply, the teenage boys bargained for turns fanning each other with newspapers or wooden-handled paper fans like those commonly used in church during long sermons. Eventually, we fell asleep only to be awakened too soon by the bell, at first feeling too drowsy to return to the day's farm chores out under the hot sun.

Supper at the usual six o'clock bell was one of my favorites: peanut butter spread on freshly-baked white bread and smothered with corn syrup.  This syrup, made in South Georgia, was donated in one-gallon containers and was usually brought home in our 1½ ton truck driven by Mr. McMillan, Farm Superintendent.  And the iced tea was just right for the occasion.

We did not have to pull weeds after supper, but were free to play baseball on the somewhat level ball field located just off the cabbage patch and adjacent to the office building where the five-member family of Mr. Durden, Superintendent, lived.  I became adept at dodging the cabbage heads while catching a big share of foul balls from my usual shortstop position.  Visions of playing professional baseball instilled in me a genuine passion for the game, and every minute was pure pleasure.

Circa 1934

**After chores there was often a quick game of football in front of the barn.**

That perfect day ended with a long, deep sleep from which we were awakened, too soon again, to begin another day of farm chores orchestrated by the ringing of the Chapel bell.

There were many such days in the unforgettable 1930s, each one offering a time for learning about and working with the wonders of God's Universe. In later years, that bell-controlled discipline would make Army life and civilian life much easier and more enjoyable.

# *Melon Head*

### James Kent

This little incident happened in about 1936 when Boy Scout Troop 16, the scout troop of the Home, spent a week at the Scout Camp. It was almost automatic. When you were promoted to the big boys' cottage, you became a member of Troop 16. We had regular meetings at the Vineville Methodist Church and attended Scout camp with other troops. However, on this occasion we were the only troop at the camp.

At camp we earned various merit badges, learned to swim, and advanced a step or two up the scout ranks. We also played a lot of pranks on each other and especially on the scout leader. Most of us even acquired a taste for goat's milk. This was necessary as it was the only milk available.

We did a few things that could be considered naughty by standards of today, but were considered boyish pranks in those days. A watermelon patch next to the camp was just too much of a temptation to let pass. It was well known that if the farmer heard us, he would come outside, holler at us, and fire his shotgun in the air. He would have a good laugh when it scared the daylights out of the raiders. There seemed to be an understanding that boys were expected to try to swipe a ripe melon or two, but do no other damage to the vines or unripened melons.

One night at nine o'clock about six of us boys decided to raid the melon patch. Evading detection from the Scoutmaster, we left camp and walked about a mile to the melon patch. Three good melons were selected and picked. We were ready to leave when something unexpected happened. For some reason one of the boys let out a yell, which brought out the farmer and his shotgun. The farmer shouted to us to get out of his melon patch and fired into the air.

Grabbing the ripe melons, we headed toward the road back to camp. There was about a four-foot drop from the field to the road below. One of the melon carriers forgot about it. He tumbled off the bank headfirst. He was not hurt as the melon hit the sandy bottom first. Then the unexpected happened: his head went into the melon! He jumped to his feet wearing the melon as a cap and ran to catch the rest of us.

At a safe distance from the field and the farmer, we stopped and turned on our flashlights to determine the extent of his injuries. The lights revealed a somewhat dizzy lad with the melon still on his head. He was known as "melon head" for the rest of the camp.

**A juicy, sweet watermelon was always a powerful temptation.**

# *Never Buy Lunch from a Home Boy*

## Van Johnson
## (Husband of Catherine Wood Johnson)

When I was a child, I lived in Macon not far from the Methodist Home. I went to Joseph Clisby School where the Home children went to school. Every day at recess a man from the Home would come to the school with a lunch cart. He would push his cart under the shade of some trees at the side of the school and distribute sacks (each containing two sandwiches) to each child. One sandwich was for lunch and one was for supper later that day.

One time my Mother did not fix me a lunch, giving me a dime instead. One of the Home boys asked, "You didn't bring your lunch?"

I said, "No, my Mother gave me a dime in order to buy my lunch." Back in those days, a dime would buy you milk and crackers for lunch.

The Home boy asked me, "Would you buy my lunch today instead of buying crackers and milk?"

I said, "Well, I reckon I would just as soon have your lunch as the crackers and milk." I gave him the dime.

I got home that day and my Mother asked me if I ate the crackers and milk for lunch that day. I said, "No, Mama, one of the boys from the Methodist Home wanted me to buy his lunch. He wanted the dime, so I bought his lunch."

My Mother told me, "Son, don't you ever do that again as long as you go to Joseph Clisby. Never buy the Home boys' lunches." She told me that was their lunch and supper and that the boys had nothing else to eat that night. She said, "That boy might have taken the dime and gone to the drug store on the way home for some ice cream and candy, but that wasn't what he needed. I am telling you, don't ever buy the Home boys' lunches again." From that day on I never did. What year was that? I would say along about 1922-23. I am now in my late 80s and live in Perry, Georgia.

I never bought lunch from a Home boy again, but on another occasion we transacted some business. In the 1920s, the children of the Home were allowed to have guinea pigs as pets. As the Great Depression worsened, the guinea pigs had to go. I came to the campus and purchased several for ten cents each. I later sold them for a dollar. Big business back in those days.

# God's Surprising Gifts

### Catherine Wood Johnson

I live a life of gratitude because God has placed in my lap some wonderful gifts.

When my parents died, I went to live with my grandparents. But when my grandfather died, my sister Edith and I were placed at the Methodist Home in 1929. I always enjoyed school and worked hard as a student. My teachers awarded me by giving me mostly A's. In those days, children had sponsors and my sponsor was the Missionary Society of the Cuthbert Methodist Church. They not only purchased clothes for me, each summer I had the privilege of visiting with them for about ten days.

When I graduated from Miller High School, the Missionary Society in Cuthbert gave me the surprise of my life. The President of the Society told me, "Catherine, we are going to send you to Andrew College if you would like to go."

In amazement, I responded, "Oh, I would love to go to college but I never dreamed I would ever have the opportunity. I figured once I graduated from school and left the Home I would have to leave, get a job, go to work and support myself." Andrew was a wonderful experience, and I will always be grateful to the Missionary Society in Cuthbert for making this happen.

In addition to the gift of college, I met a young man named Van Johnson who later asked me to be his bride. As a little girl, I told Brother J.A. Smith that I wanted him to perform my wedding when I was married. He laughed and said, "Why sure, Catherine, when the time comes, you let me know." When I was engaged, I reminded Brother Smith of his promise and he performed our wedding ceremony in the Burden Chapel on September 15, 1940. We were the first couple to be married in the Burden Chapel.

# The Amazing .22 Rifle

## James Kent

As would be expected there were no .22 rifles allowed at the Home, especially in the big boy's cottage. However, one day we had an exception.

Ernest Lawhorne, a football player for the local high school, had a bit more freedom than most boys at the Home. One day on the way home from practice he stopped at a friend's house. While there he and his friend practiced target shooting with his friend's .22 rifle. Ernest asked his friend to let him take the rifle home to show to the rest of the boys. The friend agreed, and Ernest brought the rifle home.

That night Ernest displayed his trophy to the rest of us. Although we knew what a .22 rifle was, most had never seen one much less had the opportunity to handle one. Ernest demonstrated how to aim, load, and unload the weapon. He then passed it around letting each one cock, aim, and snap the trigger. He made sure there were no rounds in the chamber.

This was not quite enough to satisfy the boys. They wanted to handle a *loaded* gun. Ernest agreed to let them do this if they would not touch the trigger. Also, we were to keep the safety on at all times. Ernest tried to check on this as each boy practiced loading and unloading the rifle. Then it happened. Someone loaded it, turned the safety off, and passed the rifle on to the next experimenter.

A shot rang out!

I do not know to this day who pulled the trigger. I do know that Alexander Martin was hit in the left shoulder. Whoever pulled the trigger dropped the rifle. Everyone backed away from Alex expecting him to be dead. He just sat there with an amazed look on his face staring at the entry point of the bullet. There was no blood and apparently very little pain. Alex did not act like it hurt and asked what we should do.  We insisted that we had to get him to the office so the wound could be cared for.  Someone asked

**The Amazing .22 Rifle**

what we were going to tell Mr. Durden, the Superintendent.

First, Alex was to tell that he was outside when he was shot and did not know from whence the shot came.  It was pointed out that nobody was allowed out at this time, and Alex would be in trouble in addition to being wounded.  Someone suggested he say that he was looking out the window and the shot came through the window.  I pointed out that the window was closed and there was not a hole in the glass.  One of the boys grabbed a shoe and busted a pane of glass.  At this time Ernest observed there was not a hole in the window screen for the round to come through.  Another boy kicked a hole in the screen and broke out half of it.  Now it looked like a shot could have come through the window pane and screen.

We began practicing our story so that we would be telling it the same way.  Each boy chose a spot to be in when the round came through the window, and then he told his story to the other boys from that perspective.  Now, we were ready to take Alex to the office so he could be treated, but a dissenter spoke up.

"Look, if a bullet came through the window, the glass would be on the inside and on the floor, not on the outer window sill."  Also, we reasoned together that a .22 shot could not break the screen and the pieces fall to the ground on the outside.  Another boy pointed out that a shot as small as a .22 shot could not make a hole as big as the one in the window screen.

We came to the conclusion it would have to be a mighty big .22 shot to do all the damage we had done to the window.  So now what?

Tell the truth.

We alerted the housemother, who did not hear the shot. (Hard to believe, but true.) We then took Alex to the office; from there he was taken to the hospital. When he came back, Alex told us that it was not a serious wound. The bullet had not penetrated very deep and had not hit a bone, nerve, or a blood vessel. The Lord was taking care of him and the rest of us.

It was an amazing evening: The fact that the rifle discharged was amazing. Our stories were amazing. The miracle that Alex was not seriously wounded was amazing. The fact that we were not punished was amazing. We will always remember the story of the amazing .22 rifle!

# A Spanking Averted

### James Kent

It started as a normal day...up at dawn, milk the cows, deliver the milk to the kitchen, and other normal chores. The last job before school was mixing cow feed. In the middle of the horse barn floor, we mixed ground hay, cottonseed meal, and molasses syrup. This was the feed that was used to keep the cows content while being milked.

All was going well until Raymond Edwards, either on purpose or accidentally, threw a scoop full in my face. I called him a few "nice names" and took a swing at him. We grabbed each other and wrestled on the floor until we fell out of the barn door. Just then Mr. McMillian, the Farm Supervisor, showed up. As I was the more aggressive one, he assumed I was at fault. He ordered us back into the barn, picked up his strap, and told me to bend over to receive a spanking.

I decided that I did not deserve a spanking and ran up the stairs to the barn loft. He followed me with the strap. I crawled through a tunnel we had made in the hay, removed some loose boards, climbed onto the barn roof, and jumped off. From there, I went to the cottage, took a shower, and began to get ready for school. Before I could finish dressing, Mr. McMillian and two hired farm hands came in the locker room. He still had the strap in his hand.

The locker room was about 18 feet wide and 30 feet long. Two rows of lockers, back to back, ran down the middle of the room. The lockers were about seven feet tall and six feet wide, which left about a yard between the top of the lockers and the ceiling. There was no way to go completely around the lockers as one end was built against the wall. The wall end of the lockers had two windows on each side. This information is important because it shapes the action that follows.

Mr. McMillian, with strap in hand, came down the side of the lockers where I was dressing, while two hired farm hands blocked the exits. A spanking was mine for sure.

Not so!

Two of the boys helped me climb atop the lockers where my pursuers couldn't reach me. I started down the other side to finish dressing, but Mr. McMillian came running. Back to the top of the lockers I scrambled and tried to descend again, but he always ran to the side I was on. So, back to the top again.

Now what? He could not get up to where I was, and I could not get down to finish dressing. To solve this problem, some of the boys began to throw my school clothes up to me. Piece by piece I was able to dress. Mr. McMillian changed his strategy. He sent the two farm hands to pull me down while he guarded the door. Even if I were able to get off the lockers, I still had to get by Mr. McMillian. It appeared that I was trapped, and a spanking was a sure thing.

Not so!

When I lured the farm hands to one side of the lockers, a friend opened the window on the opposite side and removed the screen. Some other boys gathered in a group up against Mr. McMillian. This group effectively blocked both Mr. McMillian and his henchmen. As the window was close to the top of the lockers, it was an easy step to freedom. So out I went. I jumped to the ground and was elated to be running off to school.

Now the question was, "What will happen when I arrive home from school?" To my surprise: nothing. It seemed that Mr. McMillian realized I was too old to be spanked. And I learned I was too old to fight and be disrespectful. We had a grand relationship for the rest of my days at the Home. Perseverance and help from friends are always a winning combination.

**Editor's Note:** Corporal punishment was abolished at the Home June 1, 1984, fifteen years before state licensing outlawed this practice.

# The Roaring '20s and the Depression

## Alexander A. Scarborough

From the preschool years (1924-1929), I remember the big playroom in the rear of the baby cottage. As I reflect back, I see a little red wagon, balls of all sizes, pictures in magazines, and fairy-tale books of nursery rhymes that stirred visions of future adventures. I remember the fun of sharing the toys at Christmas time and the small guns that shot a cork-on-a-string which broke all too soon and could not be repaired. I remember, too, watching the raindrops on the windowpanes, and the wonderment of learning to write my name.

Outdoor activities included catching bumblebees, playing in the sand box around the oak tree out front, taking sun baths on towels, and once viewing some spectacular shooting stars late at night.

In 1929, I started to school, and a new era of learning began. Fairy tales were more difficult to believe, and my suspicions about Santa Claus were confirmed. I had wondered how he could get around to so many houses in one night.

The Saturday morning routine of walking the six-mile round-trip to town to watch the cowboy movies at the Rialto Theater was a real treat for the group of young boys. After the field work and daily barn chores were completed, competitive activities abounded, such as football, baseball, roller-skating, scootering, card games, marble games, and rubber-ball games. An "ocean wave" merry-go-round, monkey bars, and tall swings provided many hours of pure fun and exercise.

Reaching age 12 entitled a boy to move up next door into the big boys' cottage – always a proud and enviable time. It was the beginning of the final chapter of boyhood. I was now old enough to join Boy Scout Troop 16.

In the summer of 1939, our Boy Scout Troop 16 spent a happy week at Camp Ben Hawkins. We swam three times a day, had a full schedule of other activities, and ended the week with a last-night ceremony around the campfire. The four merit badges I earned and my election as "Best Athlete" made the type of fond memories that last a lifetime. Ernie Lawhorne, another Home boy in Troop 16 and a good friend, was elected "Best All-Around."

Early in 1940, Troop 16 won third place in the regional Scout Rally held in the Macon Auditorium. Considering our handicaps (e.g., no fire-making equipment) and the large number of troops competing, we were proud to have won under such adverse circumstances.

While the Home boys were not permitted to participate in most extracurricular school activities, especially athletics, an exception was made for Ernie. He was quarterback for the Lanier High School football team and played defensive back at the University of South Carolina.

Along about this time, the Home had acquired a bus that replaced the farm truck as a mode of transportation for the children to the movies once a week and now sometimes to school. On Saturday nights, Mr. Durden would drive us to the Masonic Home to play their basketball team in the new gym with a concrete floor. On one occasion, we drove to Perry and played the junior varsity team coached by the legendary Eric Staples (over 900 wins). While I outscored (9 to 8) their star player, we lost by a close margin in the then-new zone defense style of game.

On a summer night in June 1940, the commandant of the ROTC at Lanier High, following tradition, read out the names of the upcoming seniors and the officer rank appointed to each for the following year. The rankings were based on grades and school activities. Having very little of the latter, I was somewhat apprehensive about being selected. Starting with non-coms and working upward in rank, the list reached into the second lieutenant rank before my name was called. To simply say it was an exciting moment is putting it mildly. I was ecstatic. During my senior year, I wore that officer uniform with a lot of pride.

Circa 1938

**For Alex Scarborough a solid hit always brought a smile.**

After graduating from Lanier High in June, I visited with my two sisters, Opal (and her new husband, Claude Falligant) and Ruth at Thunderbolt and spent time at Tybee Beach near Savannah. I worked the fields as usual that summer, and there was one additional task—helping to build the swimming pool behind the main building.

I remain grateful for these opportunities afforded by the Home. I only wish that Mr. Durden could have lived to see the results of the discipline and perseverance taught during those years there. I recall the day he drove me to the University of Georgia in Athens to continue my education.

# *Home Is Forever*

## Walter Scott McCleskey

Some people have a knack for saying the right thing at just the right time. Such a person was Rev. J. O. Stanalan.

From July through November, 1946, I worked at First Methodist Church in Moultrie. At that time, Brother J. O. Stanalan was Agent for the Children's Home.

Once while visiting his daughter who lived in Moultrie, he told of being accosted somewhere in South Georgia by a man who asked, "When do you turn them out?"

Brother Stanalan asked what the fellow meant. He replied, "I mean, when do you tell them they're out of the Children's Home?"

Brother Stanalan looked at the man a long time and asked him, "When do you turn *yours* out?"

# *A Childhood Remembered*

**John Darby Smith, Jr. (son)**
**for**
**J. D. (Jake) Smith**

Our father loved the Home, and he especially enjoyed the annual Labor Day reunions. His last reunion was just two months before his death at the age of 82. He particularly liked to sit on the porch of the first boy's cottage and spin yarns of his life there. He was four years old when he went there and lived in the two-story building with the slide fire escape. He milked cows and farmed. Our grandchildren loved to hear him recite all sixty-six books of the Bible; and, up until his death, he sang the hymns of the church. In fact, he sang loudly and lustily while in the hospital and invited the nurses to join in or leave. He liked to tell of marching from the Home up Vineville Avenue to Vineville Methodist Church. Each child was given one cent to put in the church offering plate. Many a penny turned up lost on that walk!

He told of volunteers coming and taking the boys to the Grand Opera House to see plays and shows and of a grand buggy (surrey-type), fringes and all, that was given to the Home. He remembered driving a mule and wagon to the freight house to pick up 100-gallon drums of apple butter. According to Father, the children had apple butter sandwiches and milk every night for supper.

He would have dearly loved to have been able to tell you his stories on film. He had a hard, harsh exterior; but, as one young friend put it, he was as soft as butter on the inside.

He became a dairy farmer and owned his own dairy.

When he died, I think he was the oldest active alumni.

Circa 1951

**After leaving the Home, "Major" John D. Smith owned his own dairy. He was voted Farmer of the Year in Bibb County.**

# *Life at the Home*

## Georgia Kent Boggs

I was placed in the Methodist Home in April of 1929. Due to health problems, I was not able to attend school the first year. Instead, I was assigned to work in the baby cottage. My job was tending to the children who were as young as four or five weeks old up to school age. Some of the babies were brought there in baskets including a set of twins, Eddie and Edna Comer. I enjoyed this work so much; it gave me a new perspective on life.

At this time I lived in the little girls' cottage with Miss Lillian Hollingsworth. There I was taught to sew, and I still do. When I was about 12 years of age, someone was needed to cut hair. Mr. Miller, who cut hair on Thursdays, taught me for about a month. After that time, I did it on my own. The wind-blown bob was in style and was cut high in the back with bangs.

At the age of 13, I went to work in the laundry for about three months, and later was moved to the little boys' cottage to work. I had two brothers there with me to help the boys from six years to about twelve. Two-piece button suits were in style as were overalls. I helped bathe and dress the boys for school and church. Two years later, I was moved to the older boys' cottage to do the ironing and mending. We had several boys in the R.O.T.C. at Sidney Lanier High School. Their uniforms had to be pressed and ready on Mondays and Fridays. On Sunday, the boys wore white linen pants and white shirts to church. It was my job to see that they were ready. I mended their clothes, so I had to keep on my toes to keep up with each boy's things.

We had our own cannery at the Home, and during the summer we had to help with the canning. Mr. McMillian would take our big truck and several boys to Perry and Fort Valley to pick up peaches. Also, we had loads of peas, beans, and butterbeans sent to us to can. The boys did the canning in gallon tin cans to be stored for the winter.

Later I worked in the milk room for several months. I had to be at this job at 5:30 A.M. as the boys were up at 5:00 A.M. to milk the cows. They would bring the milk to us in five-gallon cans that were carried on their shoulders. We strained as many as 10 to 15 cans at a time and ran the milk through a cream separator to make butter. The churn was a long flat barrel swung on hinges. We had to push and pull this until the milk turned to butter. On days that we churned, we would make about 20 to 30 pounds of butter that was later shaped to fit on plates for each table.

When Mr. and Mrs. Durden had a son, they named him Little Frankie. He had long blond curls. I tended to him for about four months. When he was two years of age, they cut his hair...and Little Frankie said goodbye to his long blond curls. I'll never forget him.

Memories of my life at the Home are rich and beautiful. I appreciate them more than words can tell. I thank God for my upbringing in such a wonderful place.

# *Fire from Heaven*

## James Kent

It all started when some of us boys discovered that we could get a little popping sound and strike a wooden match by throwing it head down on a concrete walkway.  These matches had to be ones you could strike anywhere, not the short kind that came in penny boxes.  We always had plenty of matches for lighting heaters and burning fires.  I had a pocket full most of the time.

One day at lunch, I squeezed some matches so hard that they set my pants on fire and almost burned the tablecloth in the process.  I was more careful in the future.  One would think the whole world would notice the blaze of thirty or more matches burning at once, but no one in authority saw it.  However, this is just the prelude to the story I want to tell.

We made another discovery.  If the stem of the match was split and tail fins made of paper were added, they would fly straighter and pop louder with almost 100 percent chance of igniting.  A new idea was hatched.  With the tail fins in place, we could cut a notch just behind the match head and shoot them with a rubber band.  We could get the same effect as throwing them.  This led to bolder and more audacious actions for our homemade toy.

It came to mind that we could loop several rubber bands together and increase our range.  As we made the rubber bands longer and longer, we increased the range and striking power of the flying matches.  We found that a three-foot rubber band "shooter" had a range up to 70 to 90 feet.  Now came our *pièce de résistance.*

We took the "shooter" to high school one day with plans to shoot a match from the rear of the study hall to the front.  It was about 75 to 80 feet from front to rear.  There was one professor in charge of a study hall of 100 students in the school auditorium/theater.  He had his desk placed front and center of the stage.  This placed his desk in just the right spot.  A match hitting the center of the wall above the stage curtains would drop on his desk. We knew that this would be our target and believed it would work with a few practice shots. We made a special effort to get there early while the auditorium was empty to try the "shooter." Two of the group sat on the second row from the back with four seats between them. They were the anchormen for the "shooter." The third person sat on the back row in between the other two and was to aim and fire the "shooter." After several tries, we found the range to the stucco wall above the stage. Sure enough the match struck the wall, lighted and dropped to the stage. Now for some fun.

The other students arrived, and class began. We loaded up and let go. Bulls-eye! The teacher put out the match and took a hard look at the first two rows of seats. All were innocent. He picked up his book and began reading again. Again fire came from above. There was another search and another look of innocence from all within throwing range. The teacher went back to the book with an occasional scan of the front-row students. After a short while, fire flew down again. Then the bell rang. Tomorrow would be another day.

Fire fell from heaven for the next two days. The teacher repeated his search each time, and it never occurred to him that the trouble was coming from the back row. On the third day, we fired again. By this time, the instructor knew the matches were falling from the wall above his desk. So when the first match hit his desk, he took all of the fun out of our game. He simply got up, moved his desk to the back side of the stage, and let the matches hit the floor. When they fell, he just ignored them. The challenge was ended. No more fire from heaven.

As I reflect on this adventure, the real challenge was how to deal creatively with boredom. We made a study hall into a physics lab where we learned firsthand about the design, trajectory, and flight of a wooden match. We experienced the thrill of discovery and the thrill of not being discovered.

# *To Read or Not to Read*

**James Kent**

After I became hooked on reading, I would read almost anything for enjoyment and sometimes just to learn certain things. There were two types of reading material to which I was addicted...stories of the Wild West and science fiction. These books were printed on cheap paper with a paper cover and only cost ten cents. Neither type was considered proper reading material for the youth of the Home. As a result, they had to be sneaked in and read under cover.

One day I traded my peanut butter sandwich for a book of western novels. I tried to sneak it home by placing it under my shirt held in place by my belt. I must not have hidden it very well as Mrs. Perkins, our study hall matron, observed it and asked where I had obtained such a book. I replied that I obtained it at school. Assuming that it had come from the library, she let me retain possession of it. However, being sure that this was not the type of book to be found in a high school library, she called the school the next day and found this to be true. I was properly chastised. I received a spanking and four hours of extra work while the other boys were at play, which was actually not so bad. I had finished reading the book and had traded it for another.

One of my duties after school was to start a fire in a one-hundred-pound pressure boiler that provided steam for cooking and doing laundry. On one particular afternoon, I again secretly brought home a new science fiction paperback and started the fire in the boiler. Between the times I had to add fuel to the firebox, I read the novel. I brought the pressure up to the proper point, and everything was fine. That is until I found a story that really caught my attention. I got so involved in my reading that I forgot that I had to add water and keep it at a certain level, or things could blow. Suddenly I heard a big BANG, and steam was everywhere!

Circa 1936

**James Kent (Third from Right) and Friends**

Folks came running from all over the place. Their first thoughts were about me. However, when they found that I was okay and with a dime magazine in my hand, their thoughts turned to what I had done wrong. I am thankful that I was too frightened to talk, so I did not have to confess. Since the book gave me away, I did not have to talk. I was not looking forward to what I believed would be a severe discipline. It did not materialize. A boiler inspector was called to determine the damages and the cost of repair. He informed the superintendent that the Home was very lucky that the safety plug had blown when it did, or there could have been a huge explosion causing much damage and probably killing me.

The Farm Superintendent and the older boys had to dismantle the boiler, rebuild, and reinstall it. In the meantime, we used a smaller stand-by boiler. Being smaller, it required more effort to keep the proper pressure, which left no time for reading.

To read or not to read. There are times not to.

# *A Calf for the Children's Home*

## Walter Scott McCleskey

Bishop Arthur J. Moore's oldest son, Harry, was a member of the South Georgia Annual Conference for almost 30 years prior to his death in 1969. In the early 1940s, Harry was appointed to Sandersville.

Harry told me a story of a physician living in Sandersville who had a dairy. For years the Sandersville doctor sent the Children's Home every tenth calf born to his herd. One year the tenth calf born had a deformity. Sometime later, when the calf was big enough to leave its mother, the doctor noticed its absence from the barnyard.

Circa 1931

**Only the Best for These Children**

When he asked his employees about it, they told him that they had already taken it to Macon to the Children's Home. Immediately, the doctor told his employees to select a well-formed calf, take it to the Children's Home, and return the deformed calf to their barnyard.

I will never forget that doctor's sense of stewardship.

# Care to Box?

## James Kent

This story all began when Jack Edwards called me a name.

"You're just a cockeyed blankety-blank." The "B" word I did not mind too much, but being called "cockeyed" made me see red. This word referred to a physical defect, a lazy eye as it's called today. I took one swing and hit him square in the jaw. That lick put him on the deck for about a minute. Then he came up fighting. Being somewhat more muscular and heavier than I, he was getting the best of it until the matron came in and separated us.

The next day she sent us to see Mr. Durden, the Superintendent. He talked with us for about an hour about how bad fighting was and that we had to be punished. We were told to come back tomorrow to receive our punishment because he did not know what it would be at the moment. Thinking that we would get off lightly, we went back to our cottage feeling good and were joking about the fight. Fighting did not make you enemies; it just settled an argument.

The next day promptly after school, we went to the office where Mr. Durden was waiting for us. He reached under his desk, got out a box and said, "Follow me." Not knowing what to expect, nor really caring, we trailed behind him. We were led to the basement of the small girls' cottage. There we were told to get into the coal pit. This was a concrete pit about eight feet by twelve feet and about eight feet deep. Mr. Durden showed us a leather strap about two and a half feet long. Just an ordinary spanking would be our punishment, we assumed.

Then the surprise. Mr. Durden opened the box and brought forth two brand-new pairs of boxing gloves. We were directed to put them on and prepare to fight as long as Mr. Durden thought proper. He said that we were to box until it was certain James and Jack would never have another fight while at the Home. He picked up the leather strap and instructed us to begin or he would whip us until we were ready to box.

Circa 1942

**One of these boys was looking for trouble and
found it with James Kent.**

The boxing match got under way.  In the beginning it was fun. The gloves were well padded so we could not hurt each other.  Jack and I went at it hot and heavy for about five minutes.  At this time we both came to the same conclusion:  Enough was enough, so we stopped and began to remove the gloves.

"Not enough," shouted Mr. Durden.  Picking up the strap he started down the steps.  "Get back to the boxing or bend over and get spanked until you start boxing again," he said.

So the boxing match started again.  There was not much enthusiasm now as the fun was gone.  Not many of the punches thrown ever landed.  There was a lot of foot shuffling and movement.  A lot of touching of gloves.  We must have learned to love each other as so much hugging took place. After ten minutes of this, we stopped and just looked at each other.

Once again we heard Mr. Durden shout, "Start boxing, or I start paddling." Picking up the strap, he started down the steps again. Watching his steps with care, he did not see our actions. Without a word Jack and I came to an agreement. We would meet him at the bottom of the steps and use him as a punching bag. Fortunately, this did not happen. We heard him bark, "You boys have had enough." He turned and went back up the steps. Nothing more was ever said about the ordered fight in the concrete pit. Until this day, I do not think anyone but Jack, Mr. Durden, and I knew about the surreptitious "Boxing Match."

# *Daydreams to Discoveries*

### Alexander A. Scarborough

When the stock market crashed in 1929, I was six years old. When Pearl Harbor was attacked in 1941, I was 18 years old and in my first quarter at the University of Georgia. Those 12 years of my boyhood coincided with the Great Depression of the 1930s. Those two book-end events sandwiched my discoveries of beauty and creativity found while growing up at the Methodist Children's Home.

Among my earliest memories while at the Baby Cottage (infant to six years old and now known as the Gould Cottage) is the night we kids were awakened and ushered outside to watch the falling stars, a beautiful display of bright flashes across the dark sky. In other favorite times, pictures of fairy-tale characters in books stirred my imagination, making me wish I could go with them on their colorful adventures.

Daily farm chores had few distractions, so it was natural to develop a deep appreciation and insatiable curiosity about the seasonal beauty and mysteries of nature. This was especially true on weekend afternoons spent roaming our wooded acres, filling a shoe-box with arrowheads from plowed fields and flying homemade kites in the open fields.

During those tough and fun times, there grew within me the desire to see as much of nature's beauty and wonders as future circumstances would permit. As things turned out, I was able to travel to all 50 States and 10 foreign countries where I saw more beauty and wonders than I had imagined during those bleak prospects of the Great Depression.

A favorite memory at the Little Boys' Cottage (ages 6-12) was riding on the Ocean Wave, a large merry-go-round with circular up-and-down motions of ocean waves. We sometimes went a little wild on it, pushing it to the limit of its bumps against the center pole.

Another favorite memory of mine, which took place at the Big Boys' Cottage (ages 12-18) was playing seasonal sports. On summer evenings after a six-o'clock supper, we would play baseball until it became too dark to see the usually tape-covered ball, and then lie on the grassy hillside to watch the sparkling stars appear like diamonds in the sky. I wanted to learn about their beauty and how they got scattered in those beautiful patterns so far above earth. Subconsciously, such daydreams set my course and goals in life.

The seventh grade at Joseph Clisby School (1935) was a major milestone in my life. The teacher told us about many things, but one thing I could not believe was that coal had been made from plants. On the farm, plants died and quickly decayed into dust and dirt. Another clue came from the coal we hauled in the farm truck and shoveled into the huge pit flanked by two large coal-fired boilers to generate the steam used on the campus for heating and cooking. Each cottage utilized coal in the fireplace to supplement the steam heat. On cold winter nights, while watching occasional blue flames jetting brightly from lumps of coal, I realized the reason: those blue flames were gas trapped in small-pressurized pockets inside the coal.

Freshly broken lumps of coal often revealed the multi-colored signs of traces of oil, much like those observed in spilled oil around the service stations. Putting these observations together, I believed a lump of coal had to be a lump of solidified petroleum. My course in life was set. I wanted to learn how it was possible for nature to make coal, petroleum and gas - and all other things. The decision was made to concentrate on science courses throughout high school and college so that some day the right answers could be found.

My science courses eventually led to understanding what makes the stars shine and to learning that it is the same nuclear energy that's responsible for the changing beauty and wonders of Planet Earth and all other planets, including the giant extra solar planets now being discovered at a rapid pace. I later learned that this same nuclear energy is responsible for our hydrocarbon fuels such as gas, petroleum, and coal - not fossils!

Circa 1962

**Alexander A. Scarborough spent his life in research, unlocking the secrets of the universe.**

As my knowledge increased, I began to use and combine the scientific relationships found in the works of Copernicus, Kepler, Newton, Descartes, Dutton, Einstein and other philosophers, physicists, and geologists. To bring closure to the Copernican Revolution (a complete understanding of origins of solar systems and evolution of planets and moons), the next step required finding the enigmatic solution to the Fourth Law of Planetary Motion that first had eluded Kepler in 1595.

After 16 years of trying (1980-1995), I was fortunate enough to define a solution to the final link: the Fourth Law detailing how the planets attained their orbital spacing around our Sun, all in full accord with the universal laws of physics and chemistry. These laws were made to govern all ongoing functions of an orderly, clock-like, and ever-expanding universe, and they had to have been established in the beginning by a Supreme Being.

# A Child Shall Lead Them
## (The Legacy of Ruth Ham Ferguson)

**Edwin Chase**

Ruth Ham Ferguson lived at the Methodist Home from 1933 to 1943. While she was a teenager here, there was talk and excitement at the prospect of building a gym for the children of the Home. The hope of building a gymnasium is documented in the Board notes of 1941. However, on December 7, 1941, when the Japanese bombed Pearl Harbor, they effectively bombed the plans to build a gymnasium.

During World War II, the Methodist Home sent Ruth to a secretarial school. Afterwards, she went to work for the Gulf Oil Corporation. But little Ruth Ham, with her disarming smile, carried in her heart a dream – the dream of a gymnasium for the boys and girls at the Methodist Home – a place to play, come rain or shine, freezing nights or scorching days – a place to run, play games, and just have fun.

Ruth Ham did more than dream. She went to work making her dream come true. Ruth applied herself, married, and became Ruth Ham Ferguson. She continued to work hard; and, with profit sharing and a growing economy, her little nest egg grew beyond her wildest dreams.

Her unexpected gift to the Methodist Home of one million dollars challenged the Home to revisit the challenge of 1941 and was used to launch an ambitious building project that included a state-of-the-art gymnasium, a racquet-ball court, an exercise room, a new dining room and kitchen facility, a chapel, a library and resource room, a conference center, and a suite of offices dedicated to the improvement of family life.

Ruth Ham Ferguson's legacy, the Rumford Center, will bless the lives of children, youth, and families for generations to come.

A gift of this magnitude from a former resident is a testimony to God's greatness.

Circa 1946

**Ruth Ham Ferguson did more than dream of a gymnasium for the Home. Her generous gift helped make it happen.**

Courtesy of the National Archives

**Hitler in Paris**

# Chapter Two

# *Boys Becoming Men in World War II*

It is difficult to comprehend that one day a teenage boy could be working on a farm and a few months later find himself in a foreign country carrying a rifle, leading a platoon into combat. But this scenario was the story of countless men, including 28 young men and two women from the Home.

When our boys enlisted in the armed services, they had a distinct advantage over other recruits. The Home boys all participated in a Junior Reserve Officers Training Corps at Lanier High School. Among other activities, they wore military uniforms three days a week, practiced on the drill field, honed their marksmanship and leadership skills, and became proficient at reading military maps. Because of this, one young man from the Home rose in record time from the rank of Private to Lieutenant before he hit the beach in Italy.

Our young men who served in the armed forces all agree that it was a life-transforming experience. Their stories are chronicled in the pages that follow.

# *Breakfast Delayed*

## Bill Hill

I enlisted in the Army in Macon in January of 1941 as a buck private at $21 a month. In March, I arrived in Scoffield Barracks in Hawaii and was assigned to a field artillery unit. Life was good in those days. It was the finest living conditions, best food, and the best weather I had ever experienced in my entire life. For the first time, I had a little spending money in my pockets!

That all changed on the morning of December 7 at five minutes to seven. That's when the first bomb was dropped. Having just returned from a field exercise on Saturday, I was relaxing that Sunday morning. My friend, Norm Parrish, had called to me, "Hey, Bill, get up. Let's go get some eggs. It's going to be a long time 'til lunch." Truer words were never spoken. It was a very long time until lunch – about 17 hours later!

When we first heard the bombs exploding, we thought it was a practice exercise. With a shocked expression and surprise in his voice, a private explained, "Those planes are from the Empire of Japan!" The sounds of bombs grew louder and louder. The Japanese were bombing Wheeler Field! We dressed in our field gear, headed to the review field, and took cover. Later we loaded artillery shells on trucks and went to our field positions. I could see the burning buildings at Wheeler, but I did not realize how bad the situation was at Pearl Harbor.

I saw Pearl Harbor for the first time two weeks later. I was aghast at the still smoldering harbor littered with ships protruding partly out of the water. The reality of war with its demands and sacrifices ended my idealistic life and launched me on an unforgettable journey.

Courtesy of the National Archives

**USS Shaw Exploding at Pearl Harbor**

## *An Unforgettable Turning Point Day*

**Wiley J. Kent**

October 20, 1940, began as any other day did at the Home. We older boys arose at 6:00 A.M. After completing our assigned chores, we went to breakfast. After breakfast we dressed for school.

Four of us were called to the office. Mr. Durden, the Superintendent, told us that we were going to join the military. "When?" we asked. *"When?"* He assured us that it would be this day.

He called Mr. McMillian, the Farm Supervisor, and instructed him to take us to the recruiting office in the car. On the way to the recruiting office, we were given the choice of the Army, Navy, or the Marines. We chose the Navy for no real reason other than it was a choice we had to make. Mr. McMillian took us to the Navy office. Except for James, we all passed the physical exam without any problems. The Navy doctor was concerned about James's eyes as he was wearing glasses. After a closer look at James's eyes and the glasses he was wearing, he asked James if he knew the best thing he could do with the glasses. James said, "No. What?"

The doctor said, "Throw them out the window." James did not wear glasses for the next 22 years.

The Naval recruiting officer said that the Navy would accept all three of us. There was a small hitch though. The Navy could not accept us for three months. Their quota of enlistees was filled for that period of time.

We were loaded back into the car and were driven directly to the recruiting offices for the Marines. After reviewing the Navy's medical exam, the officer said the Marines would be glad to have us. Then he dropped a bomb. He told Mr. McMillian that after he signed the papers the Marines would be at the Home in *three weeks* to pick us up and transport us to the appropriate Marine base.

We were again loaded into the car and taken to the Army recruiting office. After a very quick physical exam, the Army recruiter said that he thought that we would make very good soldiers since we had a higher education than most recruits. Before the recruiting sergeant filled out the induction papers, Mr. McMillian asked him when he could take us into the Army. The sergeant responded, "Today." I think my heart skipped a beat. The papers were signed at once.

We were immediately taken home where we packed two sets of underwear, two pairs of socks, and an extra change of clothing. After that, we were taken back downtown where we purchased a set of shaving articles, soap, and several towels. Mr. McMillen then gave each of us fifty cents and turned us over to the Army recruiters.

That night we slept in the barracks at Fort McPherson in Atlanta, Georgia. That day was a turning point for each of us, launching us toward incredible experiences that would change our lives forever.

# A Surprise Encounter Far from Home

## Bill Hill

In June of 1930, I arrived at the Methodist Home as an eight-year old at a time when our country was in the midst of the Great Depression.  However, as an eight-year old, I frankly was not aware of any depression.  On my first full day at the Home, I found myself picking tomatoes and piling them in a wheelbarrow with a boy named Roy Massey who had a brother named Calvin.  We worked most of the morning picking tomatoes together and taking them to the kitchen where the older girls were washing and slicing them, preparing for our next meal.  There was always a quiet hour after lunch and play time after that.

Twelve years after I arrived at the Children's Home, I found myself in the middle of a world war.  I was resting in a tent on the Island of Leyte in the South Pacific struggling with a high fever caused by malaria.  Across the tent, I recognized a fellow that looked like Roy Massey, the lad I met my first day at the Children's Home.  I made my way to Roy and asked him if he had heard from his brother, Calvin.  Shocked, he said, "You know my brother?!"

"Yeah, I grew up with him at the Children's Home in Macon," I responded.  That's all I needed to say.  Roy was shocked that I was the boy who had picked tomatoes with him years earlier.  We talked all that day every chance that we had as Roy was eager to catch up on old times and find out what was happening.  He was serving as a medic in the Thirty-Fourth Infantry Regiment.  After the war, Roy became a prominent pharmacist in California.

Roy Massey and I picked tomatoes together as small boys.  We went to the same school.  We both served in the Army and found ourselves under the same tent on the Island of Leyte in the South Pacific.  What are the chances of this happening?  Our similar circumstances served to strengthen our friendship.  Life threw us together, flung us to the other side of the world and brought us back together again. War does strange things.

**First Flag on Guam**
**(Symbolic of Two Friends Meeting Far From Home)**

**Note from Dr. Steve L. Rumford, President/CEO:** I have always been amazed that the minutes of the Trustees of the Home clearly reported the severe shortages and difficulties the Home faced during the Depression. Yet the residents have told me many times they *did not know* of the Depression as a time of hardship until after they left the Home. Like any good parent, the Home made those issues adult issues and shielded the children from further hardships.

# *Mission Accomplished*
# *(But Not What I had in Mind)*

### James Kent

I landed in Italy on October 11, 1943. Days later I was called to the regimental headquarters for a briefing. I knew that it was something important as platoon leaders are not usually briefed by regimental commanders. I was informed that I would take my platoon and ford the Vulturno River in the British sector and make sure that the German forces saw the American uniform. The plan was to make the Germans believe that the main effort to obtain a bridgehead over the Vulturno would be made by the British forces aided by the American Army. Therefore, the Germans would commit their reserves to the British sector. This would enable the American forces upriver to create a bridgehead before the Germans could redeploy their reserves. My platoon was to cross the river before daylight on October 13th. (The main assault would begin three hours later.) The briefing ended with these final words from my regimental commander, "Come back if you can."

At 5:30 A.M., a smoke screen was laid down to cover our crossing and convince the Germans a major effort to ford the river had begun. About halfway to the river, a German mortar barrage hit the middle of our platoon, wounding three. The river was much deeper than anyone had expected, causing us to lose our best radio and walkie talkie. And half of my platoon didn't even reach the other side.

After crossing the river, the smoke was so thick I could only see about 30 feet ahead. Reaching a small rise, we discovered that the Germans had already retreated leaving behind some maps, equipment and personal items which led me to believe that they were planning to return. Almost as soon as we had established a defensive perimeter we could hear the enemy approaching. They were stumbling and calling to each other as the smoke made it difficult to see.

Courtesy of the National Archives

**American Troops in Similar Areas as Kent**

It appeared the soldiers were planning to occupy their old positions, not suspecting that we were there. Three German soldiers walked into our perimeter and quickly surrendered when our forces stood up from their old foxholes. They were quickly disarmed and escorted to the rear by two of my men. A few minutes later, we captured three more prisoners. When I noticed the sky was becoming brighter and the smoke thinning, I positioned a two-man listening post about fifty yards in front of our defensive position. After about twenty minutes they returned to report the approach of a much larger enemy force.

When the Germans came within sight it was obvious they expected trouble as they carried their weapons at the ready. We waited until the men in front had no place to hide and opened fire. The leading three hit the ground and due to our fire could not return fire. Those in the rear turned and ran. When the fire fight was over, the three trapped German soldiers were told to surrender, which they did somewhat unwillingly. They were disarmed, searched and dispatched to the rear.

Suddenly a burst of automatic fire hit the parapet of my trench. I dove for cover. Then a second burst. This time the rounds were hitting in the trench about six inches from my face. I can still see the tracer rounds spewing and uncovering a hand full of bullets a few inches from my nose. The second burst of fire convinced me that it was time to move as I had become the obvious target. I called for covering fire from my men. I was out just in time as the next burst from the machine gun sprayed the entire trench.

I spotted cover on the left flank and took a firing position. From there I could see under the trees to my left that enemy forces were trying to outflank us. I directed the soldier nearest me to shift his fire to the left to stop their advance. After a second burst of fire, things were quiet for a few moments.

My men began to fire sporadically at targets of opportunity. When I turned my attention to the front, trying to determine what was drawing their fire, a voice behind me called out, "COMRADE." Looking to the rear I saw a German soldier, about ten to twenty yards away, with a light machine gun pointed at my back. There were two other German riflemen with him. As I started to turn and face him, he raised his weapon and said sternly, "Halt, Comrade!" I knew my number was up. I could surrender or die.  I dropped my weapon and raised my hands.  He indicated that I should order my men to cease fire and at the same time called his soldiers forward.  I knew there were only two choices for me: order a cease fire or watch my men die.  I chose to order the cease fire.

Courtesy of the National Archives

## American Prisoners of War in the Same Situation as James Kent

The Germans quickly disarmed us and destroyed our weapons.  We were lined up and began marching to the enemy's rear.  As we started to move, I took a good look at my men.  I saw deep sadness in each face.  I thought that this was how I must look to them.  My thoughts were that we had failed our nation.  I was in command, so it had to be my fault.  Then I recalled the instructions from the regimental commander: "Make sure the Germans see the American uniform and come back if you can."  I reminded the men that our primary purpose was to be seen by the enemy, and that had been accomplished. Returning to our lines was not that vital to our mission. We had taken about as many German prisoners as the Germans had when we were forced to surrender.

I learned later that our mission had succeeded in luring the German reserves to the British sector. This allowed the American forces upriver to create a bridgehead across the Vulturno River with fewer casualties. If we were able to save one life, our capture was worth it.

**Editor's Note**: The first telegram received by the Methodist Home from the War Office stated that James Kent was missing in action. Several months later a second telegram arrived indicating that James Kent had been located.

# *When I Needed It Most – A Message of Hope*

## **James Kent**

Several weeks after my capture by German forces in Italy, I found myself in a POW Camp in Germany, *Stalag VII A*. My cell was six feet by eight feet with a ten foot ceiling. There was one window about ten feet high that was whitewashed to keep prisoners from seeing outside. My first day in solitary was not too bad, but as I continued to give only my name, rank and serial number, my living conditions were gradually made much more uncomfortable. During the day, I was kept in a bare cell with a heater that came on just long enough to keep my hopes up. Rations were reduced to bread and water once a day. Finally, they took my straw mattress. All I had were the slats to sleep on. To say the least, after several weeks, I was feeling very low.

I needed something to lift my spirits.

One day, after returning from my bare cell to my regular cell, I looked around to see if there had been any changes. Everything was just as I had left it. Then looking up at the whitewashed window, I noticed some scratches in the whitewash that I had not seen before. When I looked at the window at a new angle, I could see that the scratches were symmetrical and uniform. I thought it might be writing of some kind. So, I decided to investigate further. Turning my cot on its end and using the slats as ladder rungs, I climbed up to inspect this new found phenomenon.

The message was handwritten in script. At first, the script did not make any sense to me. Each letter had numerous curls, loops and squiggles. Then I recalled reading a poem written in Old English script in high school. I could read each letter but the writing was on the *outside* of the window which made it a mirror image. (Everything was written from right to left.) After learning to read the script a letter at time, I was impressed by the beauty of the writing. It was as if the writer, skilled in calligraphy, had taken great pains to make sure that each letter was perfect. The thought came to me that the writer used the Old English format to deceive the guards into believing it was just scratches in the whitewash. Anyway, the inspirational message I discovered was the following:

> So you think you are alone in there.
> Remember what Jesus said in Matthew.
> "Lo, I am with you always, even until the
> end of the world." He is there with you.
> The Germans might kill you but they can't
> eat you. You will be in heaven with Jesus!

I believe the comment about being eaten was an effort at humor. The rest of the message I took very seriously as it helped me to cope with what I was to face in the days to come. But I wonder why it took me several weeks to notice this message or was it written just when I needed it most? God's grace was sufficient for me. It was comforting to know that although I was in solitary confinement, I was *not* alone.

# *Freedom at Last!*

## James Kent

On the morning of January 23, 1945, I was a prisoner of war deep in Germany.  We awoke to find that sometime during the night the German guards had left us.  Several officers were seen moving across country toward the Russian lines.  We could hear the big guns in the distance.  A Polish woman who frequently brought us food told us that the Russians were only five kilometers away.  I had my hopes up briefly before new guards arrived – the dreaded SS troops.

About a week later we awoke to find that a tank column from General Patton's Army was on the hill overlooking the camp.  The German Commander offered a flag of truce and after a brief consultation surrendered the camp.  Because our camp was well behind the German lines, the tank column Commander wanted to leave as soon as possible.  He knew that the column would be trapped if he lingered.  As many of the POWs as possible boarded the tanks and half tracks and moved out.  We rode all night looking for a means to return to friendly lines.  Every road we tried was blocked by mines, blown bridges, or superior tank forces.  The German tanks had guns that outranged our tanks and fired before our tanks could move into effective range.  I can still see those white hot rounds flying by us.  No one was hurt and no tank was hit.  It was an all-night ride and ended just where it began  - on a hill overlooking the camp!  So with no gas to keep running and outgunned by the German tanks, the Commander of the tank force surrendered, and we were POWs again.

A few days later, our stay at *OFLAG XIIIB* came to an abrupt end as we were marched to a waiting train and boarded for a two-day ride to Nuremburg.  After three days, we began a walking tour.  On the third day we were marching in a steady rain.  I tried to remain dry by draping a sheet on a stick over my head.  It kept some of the rain off and kept me somewhat warm. I think I actually went to sleep and some of the other POWs guided me along. I remember waking up as we moved off the road in the dark and did not recall anything from about noon until the time we left the road for the night. During this time period I lost the heel off my left boot and one of my buddies picked it up and gave it to me when we halted for the night. For the next two days I had to walk without a heel. By the time I was able to get a farmer to fix it, I had a very sore foot, which still bothers me at times.

This journey turned into a 90-mile "foot tour of Germany." One day on this tour we had a real scare. It was a clear bright spring morning. A day joyous to behold. There was a cloudless blue sky, and it seemed we could see forever. For some reason I looked up and saw an American fighter circling high overhead. Suddenly the day was not so beautiful. It was obvious the pilot could see only a column of soldiers in formation marching down a

Courtesy of the National Archives

**The Possibility of Friendly Fire**

highway. A hasty effort was made to alert the pilot that we were POWs, not a combat unit. Using rolls of toilet tissue we tried to write POW in an open field so the pilots would know who we were and not attack. But we were too late. They began to peel off for a firing pass, and the first aircraft began its run. He came in, fired a short burst, then recognized that we were not German troops. He pulled up sharply wagging his wings to call off the attack. He succeeded as the pilots following just buzzed us and flew off.

We arrived at *Stalag VIIA* on April 20th. We were liberated on April 29th.

We were free again but not totally out of harm's way. While awaiting transportation just outside an airport, three German jet fighters streaked overhead. We ran for cover. However before the air defense could fire, the German pilots actually flew their planes onto the airstrip wagging their wings. When the excitement settled down, we finally boarded a plane for France.

Upon landing, there was a pleasant surprise. We were given a scrumptious dinner. The meal, my finest in two years, was delicious in every respect. I had forgotten how good food could taste. Our reception in France was made even better when General Eisenhower took the time to shake hands with all of us.

Now there was no doubt. We were FREE, FREE, FREE!!!

# The 1940s:  Sentimental Years of College and War

## Alexander A. Scarborough

One of my fondest memories came in a letter from the University of Georgia offering a one-year tuition scholarship as a result of my SAT score in the upper two percent group.  My long-time dream was finally within reach.  Mr. Durden and I agreed that it would be possible for me to work in Athens to earn the living expenses.  To a naïve country boy, the future seemed rosy and exciting.

The weather that September day in 1941 seemed perfect while riding with Mr. A.C.  Durden, Home Superintendent, to enroll at the University of Georgia in Athens.  I enrolled and signed up for the National Youth Administration work program at 25 cents per hour.  Just two blocks off campus, I found living quarters where the cost for a small room with two roommates and two meals a day was $15 a month.  At the time, a full-course Sunday lunch could be had for 35 cents, all-inclusive. Tuition was $47.50 per quarter which was covered by my SAT scholarship for the freshman year only.  The economics looked good; I had arrived in paradise to learn and to enjoy.

The Japanese bombed Pearl Harbor on December 7, 1941, very near the end of my first quarter of study at Georgia. Otherwise, my freshman year went well.  I made the Dean's List, lettered on the freshman basketball team, and pole-vaulted on the freshman track team.  I went to my first dance where a nervous decision to break in on any coed required about 1½ hours.  Relief came when I broke in on Wilma and discovered that dancing was easy and fun.  It became habitual on most weekends.  Many times there were swinging big bands of the era in person…Glenn Miller, Benny Goodman, etc.  I remember Doris Day when she sang with Les Brown; she talked with some of us during breaks.

The draft situation allowed science students to stay in school provided we took accelerated courses. My overloads of study each quarter reduced my athletic activities to cross-country racing, winning a gold medal in the 5K intramural race, and making the all-star softball team at shortstop. But the university allowed me to graduate one year early, on June 7, 1944, the day after D-Day in Europe. Having received my draft notice several weeks earlier, I prepared to report in July for military service. Barely holding back the tears when saying good-bye to Mr. Durden and my home for 20 years, I took the train to Fort McPherson, Atlanta, for induction into the Army. I was assigned to infantry training.

Basic training was at Camp Wheeler in Macon. After 16 weeks of intensive training, followed by some R&R time, we boarded the troop transport, *Sea Fiddler,* somewhere on the Maryland coast. Thirteen days later we landed in Naples under the shadow of Mount Vesuvius, still smoking from its eruption early in the year. It was a beautiful sight on that cold 23$^{rd}$ day of December, just two days before a lonesome Christmas of getting acclimated to the deep mud which covered an otherwise beautiful, but partially bombed, Italian countryside.

For the next eight months, I was busy with additional training in a replacement depot at Casserta and directing the traffic of POW German soldiers to internment areas. I served my last two months as a Combat Engineer preparing to invade Japan. This was after Germany had surrendered, and President Roosevelt had died in office. Building a pontoon bridge across the Po River was the main training event.

Early in August we boarded the ship to invade Japan via the Panama Canal. As we boarded, we were handed *The Stars & Stripes* issue with *Atom Bomb!* as the screaming headline. In the middle of the Atlantic, the bigger news arrived: Japan had surrendered after the second atomic bomb had been dropped. It was a happy shipload of soldiers, especially when the ship was diverted from its original destination and anchored in Boston Harbor under a full moon...another beautiful sight!

Courtesy of the National Archives

**The Stars & Stripes published an issue with "Atom Bomb!"**

A month later, I married a girl that I met while in basic training. We were married in the Burden Chapel on the Home campus in Macon. My Army discharge papers came in July, 1946; two years of service were over, and thanks to the atomic bomb, I was alive and ready to begin a career in chemistry, research, and development. I worked 14 months with Swift & Co. in Atlanta before yielding to my first love - learning. Using the GI Bill of Rights at Georgia Tech, I earned a degree in Chemical Engineering. This education gave me a broader knowledge of the basics needed for life's purposes. It later proved to be a wise decision.

Courtesy of the Middle Georgia Archives, Washington Memorial Library, Macon, GA, circa 1953

**"Buddy at Bat"**

# Chapter Three

## *Never a Dull Moment on the Farm*

Working on a farm is often fraught with adventure (which provides fertile ground for great stories) especially when the farm hands are primarily teenage boys. The Methodist Home had a dairy with approximately thirty head of cattle. In addition to cows, there were mules, pigs and chickens. There was a hayloft for playing hide and seek and a horse to ride if you could catch him. The farm animals, like the weather, were unpredictable. This was the glory of working on a farm: No two days were ever the same. There was always something unexpected.

These stories begin in the early 1930s and end in the early 1960s when the farm was shut down. They illustrate the truth that on a farm a surprise awaits around every corner.

Circa 1938

**"Pups with Kittens"**

# *Milking Chores*

## Bill Chase

My eyes were opened, but it was still dark. The words nudged at me again, "Wake up, Billy. We've got to get the cows." It was 4:30 in the morning and stark black outside. How can anyone awaken so early, I wondered.

"Okay, I'm getting up," I said struggling to get the words out. Charles flipped the lights on. I ducked my head to escape the brightness and looked up squinting into his face.

"We'll leave as soon as you get dressed. Oh, don't forget your flashlight." He was off as silently as he came.

I scratched my head and yawned like an old barn cat. As I dressed, I remembered how much I had looked forward to the day when I would be a "barn boy" and old enough to help with the milking of the cows.

About the age of ten, the boys at the Children's Home began participating in the farm's chores. This day was the first of an evolution of many new experiences. While I can say I never enjoyed farm work, that first day was a grand initiation into the "starting to grow up world."

Pulling weeds and being a barn boy were among the first chores assigned to those who had come of age. Most of the farm work and yard work were drudgery, but getting the cows to the barn was an adventure. It was by far the most important work to be done because there would be no milking without the cows. And it was never certain where the cows would be found. They could be as far away as the pasture near Pierce Avenue or the one closer to Vista Circle. The cows would occasionally stray beyond their fenced pastures—as when they broke the fence and got into Mr. Bowen's camellias. Sometimes an unknown element could create a surprise—as when a skunk was discovered before the cows were found. These were the reasons the flashlights were handy.

In time, getting the cows became less an adventure and more a necessity. The cows had to be milked twice a day—before breakfast and before supper. It was always a mystery to me why the cows would come to the barn for the afternoon milking, but you always had to find and herd them to the barn in the morning. I guess cows have a hard time getting their day started, just as many people do.

**Catching "Rollie" in the early morning and rounding up the cows made you feel like a real cowboy.**

After you herded the cows to the barn, each one to be milked was put into her individual milking stall complete with a head-retaining collar to keep her there. Stalls were on a common concrete floor and were separated from each other by stout metal railings. The two barn boys also had the job of cleaning the cow's sides and udders in preparation for the boys assigned as milkers. Each stall had its own feed trough, and a half-bucket of the choicest feed was given to each cow before the milking started. The feed was supposed to keep the cows contented, but sometimes that was not sufficient.   Many a cow kicked over the milking bucket or stepped into it.   When that happened it was time to start over.

Working as a barn boy was a wonderful preparation for life. In those early years I began to develop a work ethic that has served me well throughout my life.   I still am an early riser.   I'm just grateful I don't have to go looking for cows every morning.

# A Pain in the Butt

## James Kent

Every year in the late summer the older boys of the Home were required to prepare silage for cow feed during the winter. This was hard work and greatly dreaded. Large fields of corn and special grass had to be cut by hand and hauled by two horse wagons to the silage grinder. We used machetes to cut the corn and grass, which was then picked up by hand and loaded onto the wagons. The work was hot and sweaty. In order to protect ourselves from being cut by the leaves of the corn and grass, we wore long sleeved shirts.

Cutting the corn was not too bad as the fields were open, and we were cutting single stalks of corn. One swing of the machete and it was done. However, the grass was a different story. It grew in large clumps with up to 50 stalks. Each stalk was up to ¾ of an inch thick. There was another disadvantage to harvesting this grass. The clumps made good homes for yellow jackets, wasps, and other stinging insects. The rule of thumb was to approach with care or get stung several times a day, usually by more than one insect at the same time.

We boys learned early that when you agitated a nest of yellow jackets, it was best to fall flat on your face at once. This action caused the insects to fly over you onto the next nearest victim. With this maneuver, there were very few stings, if any. Mr. Camp, our farm manager, observed this defense against the yellow jackets, and thought it was superb. He even tried to use it himself one day.

While Mr. Camp was walking by a clump of grass being cut, out came a large swarm of yellow jackets. We boys dropped to the ground at once. The yellow jackets flew over us and straight toward Mr. Camp. Now I must tell you that Mr. Camp was a very large man, especially around the middle. He went down, but only got on his knees and elbows. In this position, his backside made a very large target.

About ten or twelve yellow jackets hit each side of his rump. I assure you he then got absolutely flat on the ground in spite of his size. But it was too late. He learned the meaning of a real pain in the butt.

Circa 1937

**Working in a Corn Field**

# A Prayer for Buttercup

## Edwin Chase

On the dairy farm where I worked as a 12 year-old boy, I had a favorite cow named Buttercup. She was in trouble, and the aftermath of her misfortune would cause me to ponder for years, leaving an indelible imprint upon my life.

As I walked through the huge wooden doors of the barn, out of the corner of my eye I saw something that drew my attention. Buttercup's right eye looked gruesome as it appeared to be partly out of its socket, and fluid oozed down her matted coat. I wondered if she had snagged it on some barbed wire. Deeply concerned, yet keeping my feelings to myself, I panicked when I heard the Farm Superintendent, Mr. Lanier, tell someone that he was calling the veterinarian to remove Buttercup's injured eye in order to protect her remaining healthy eye.

That evening when I went to bed, I pulled the covers over my head. The sadness and tears that had been welling up inside me poured forth. When I could catch my breath, I began to pray. I prayed and cried, pleading with God to save Buttercup's eye. As my prayers went to heaven, I went to sleep.

The next morning as I was doing my barn chores, I saw Mr. Lanier scratching his head and heard him say to one of the workers, "I'll have to call Doc Johnson and tell him not to come." I wondered about his statement and made my way to Buttercup's stall and stood directly in front of her. I found myself staring into a perfect set of huge brown eyes. Not a trace of dried mucous marred her beautiful golden coat. It was as if the injured eye had been replaced by a perfectly healthy one. I was speechless and overwhelmed with a flood of conflicting feelings washing over me: shock, relief and confusion. Fearing ridicule, I dared not say a word to anyone about my tearful intercessions the previous night. The whole experience was too big for me. Although I did not mention the incident to anyone for many years, the memory has become a part of me.

I have read about and researched the subject of prayer and healing for nearly four decades. And, a few years ago, I had the opportunity to do some informal research on my own. I discussed with Mr. Lanier, the Farm Superintendent, the mysterious experience of Buttercup's healing more than 40 years ago. He recalled the cow's serious injury and the unanswered questions everyone had regarding the healing and restoration of her right eye. As we talked and shared our memories, a long moment of silence stretched between us. We found ourselves reflecting on a gracious God who hears the prayers of children.

# The Chicken House

## Charlie Gordon

Growing up in the Home I particularly remember that I always loved fried chicken and shiny shoes.

This caper happened when I was about thirteen or fourteen. All the boys my age were assigned a chore for a period of three, perhaps six, months. At the time my chore was the "Chicken House"...or feeding the chickens.

Every morning before going to school, I had to make sure the chickens had food and water. I really didn't mind the job; it didn't take long and took little effort. But anyone who has worked with chickens would agree that boots are needed for the job, and I didn't have any.

I came up with what I thought was a great plan to get a pair of boots. I got up at about two o'clock one morning, dressed, and went to the chicken house. In the chicken house, there were six water faucets about four or five inches high coming out of the ground on each side. I removed all the water pans from each side and cut the faucets on so each would have a slow steady stream running directly on the floor. I then returned to my building and got back in the bed. I wanted to create a huge puddle on the floor. Unfortunately, we had a hard freeze that night.

The next morning, the Farm Superintendent was at the chicken house before I arrived. It seemed about two hundred chickens had smothered by piling on top of each other in an attempt to get away from all the ice and water.

In one fell swoop, we had plenty of chicken to eat, and the chicken-house job was stepped up a notch. I lost my chicken house job and was put on restriction, but I was the one that made feeding chickens at the Methodist Home fun. Rubber boots were bought that same day for the lucky boy who replaced me at the chicken house.

# *Toasted Oats*

## Bill Chase

This was the big day—the day we would use the new combine to harvest oats on the forty-acre plot of bottom land next to the Ocmulgee River.

Mr. Rene Lanier, the Farm Superintendent, loaded five of the older boys into the ¾-ton flatbed truck and drove us to the oat field located on the bottom land. We had seen the combine the day before when we hitched it to the John Deere tractor. It had taken four boys to lift the combine's tongue to the tractor's tow bar. On the day before, Mr. Lanier had arranged for someone to drive the tractor, with the combine in tow, to the field so it would be ready for the day's work.

Mr. Lanier gave us our assignments. He drove the tractor that pulled the combine while Charles and I worked the combine. My brother Buddy, J.W., and David worked the field. The combine picked up the oat tares and threshed out the oats as the tractor pulled it back and forth in the field. Charles and I sat side-by-side on the combine. Charles bagged the oats as they came out of the chute, and I tied the burlap sack with a heavy cord and tossed the filled bag down the combine's slide to the barren field. The other boys loaded the filled sacks onto the truck.

The work went well at first. Charles, sitting on the inside seat, hooked the sacks to the chute and quickly replaced a filled sack for an empty sack. I tied the mouth of the sack as it was removed from the chute and tossed the sack down the slide. We had the operation down pat after three passes over the field—or so we thought!

One of the empty burlap sacks that Charles tried to use had a large tear in the side. "This one is no good," he shouted over the machine noise. "Get rid of it," he said as he passed it to me. I folded the sack in half and placed it under my seat. This was a crucial mistake. I did not realize the combine's motor was immediately below where I was sitting. We continued working without incident—for a while.

The day was hot and dusty, and the smell of oats filled the air. "Ah, the smell of Merita bread," I said in a jovial way.

"Merita bread, no way!" shouted Charles. "You've got a fire under your butt!" he blurted as he pushed me off the seat and quickly followed—half falling and half sliding down the bag slide. Just before I went sprawling off the combine, I saw Mr. Lanier's head turned back at us. His mouth was opened in fright, and he was saying something. When I hit the ground, I realized Mr. Lanier had stopped the tractor; he had seen the fire, too—probably before we did. The other boys ran to the combine to give assistance.

In a few seconds, the surrounding ground, especially behind the combine was ablaze. The speed of the spreading fire was unbelievable. "All of you get way out of the way," commanded Mr. Lanier as he herded us about 100 feet away from the burning oat field. "That gas tank is going to blow," warned Charles.

Once Mr. Lanier saw all the boys were safe, he did a remarkable thing. He said, "All of you stay here. I mean it." He bolted back to the tractor, lifted the combine's heavy tongue with one hand and pulled the connecting pin from the tractor's tow bar with his other hand. He climbed on to the tractor and drove it to safety.

In the midst of all this, another remarkable thing happened: The engine of the combine never stopped running and the engine fan kept blowing the fire away from the combine. So, with the tractor out of harm's way and the combine seemingly taking care of itself, we returned and fought the fire with a vengeance. Armed only with burlap bags, we beat the fire out completely. It was quite a battle. When it was all over, there was a huge blackened area the size of the infield of a baseball diamond. We were all exhausted but relieved.

As we were leaving the field, I felt a sense of pride as well as loss. As boys, we had faced a serious crisis and responded with courage and determination. No one was injured, and the machinery was not seriously damaged. Quick thinking and a team effort saved the day. All the boys were safely returned home. Unfortunately, Mr. Lanier had the worst wrenched back of his life.

# Excerpts from *An Autobiography*

## Wallace L. Hubbard

I was born on July 31, 1923, to Ernest Hubbard and Werta Bray Hubbard of Albany, Georgia. I was the middle child of three children. My father died of tuberculosis in 1926. My grandmother died in 1929, and my mother was killed in an automobile accident while en route to her mother's funeral. Shortly thereafter my brother and I were placed at the Methodist Home.

There was no shortage of enjoyable activities for young or older children: swings, skating, scooters, cowboys and Indians, "Simon Says," homemade telephones, pop guns and rubber guns. The older group, though still too young for real work, would be used in the silos to stomp down and compact the silage (chopped corn stalks) as it was directed into the silo from a chute above. When the boy directing the chute heard an ear of corn in the chute, he would aim at one of us below. I had my share of hits on the "noggin."

Every child attended public school. Elementary school was Joseph Clisby School. We walked to and from school. I remember the first time I ever saw snow. The teacher allowed us to stand at the window and watch the snowflakes fall and dissipate into the grass.

We also attended church every Sunday at Vineville Methodist Church. We were dressed in our best clothes, and each of us would drop two pennies in the collection plate.

When I was old enough, I started working on the farm that was managed by Mr. McMillan. My first chore was hoeing in the field where I met Mr. Gen Lucas, a black farm worker who taught us the basics of farming. He was the father of eighteen children and regularly entertained us with stories about his family members. The oldest offspring was a sophomore in college.

Corn was the main crop and demanded the most work, especially at the end of the summer season. The corn stalks were cut, hauled to the barn, and stored in the silos for feed for the cows.

In the fall, we played rough and tough football games. In a rare case three of us, John Lawhorne, Jackson Shannon, and I, were permitted to play for a neighborhood team in a city-wide football league. John was the flashy halfback, and Jackson and I were linemen. Our team won the Central Georgia championship defeating the heralded Macon Y.M.C.A. team.

There were the seasonal outings that we looked forward to with excitement. In the summer, there was the "Sunshine Special", a day in the park for swimming, boating, and picnicking. I had always been afraid of the water and would just dunk my head into the water to make believe I had been under the water. That is until a younger boy shamed me into diving off of the diving board. *I nearly broke my neck.*

In the fall, the State Fair and circus came to town. While attending my first circus, I was thrilled and astonished when Tom Mix entered with his show.

On Saturday afternoon, we were permitted to walk into town and go to the movies. Movies in those days consisted of sing-a-longs, cartoons, weekly serials, and main features (silent black & white). The main movie was usually a Harold Lloyd, Charlie Chaplin, or The Keystone Cops.

During my later years, I was assigned to a few special duties. For openers, I was chosen to announce morning reveille by producing 100 gongs on a large liberty-type cast iron bell. It took every 120 pounds of my weight to push the bell. I don't know why I was chosen except maybe because someone had noticed that I was usually an early riser. In conjunction with the wake-up call, in the winter I would start two gas-heating furnaces.

I was especially privileged to enjoy a week's vacation at the Edwin Gould (of the nationally famous Gould family) Foundation Camp at Windham, New York, in the Catskills Mountains. I was one of ten children selected from different orphanages in South Georgia.

Circa 1948

**When we were not at the movies,
we could pretend to be stars.**

I graduated from high school in 1941 six months after the bombing of Pearl Harbor. But my years at the Home had prepared me well for the challenges that lay ahead.

# The Piggies Paid the Fair's Fare

### James Kent

One year our best brood sow gave birth to twelve piglets. A group of us were there to witness this event; and, as each piglet was born, Mr. McMillian handed it to one of us saying that the piglet belonged to the holder. We all believed that each piglet was our very own – to have and to care for.

When the fair came to town, one other boy and I were not allowed to attend. While all the other boys were at the fair, we plotted to take our piglets and sell them for money for the fair. Selling the piglets was much easier than we had expected as the first farmer we approached bought them for 75 cents each. We were sure we had made a good deal and could hardly wait for night to come.

As soon as it was dark, we dressed and sneaked out to the fair. We rode the electric trolley which was only two blocks from the Home. Once there, we attached ourselves to some adults who had paid to get in and just walked in with them – no tickets. We spent our money quickly, saving only a nickel for the trolley ride home. Once home, we returned to bed without being caught. Oh, but it did not end there!

The next day, Mr. McMillian noticed that the piglets assigned to us were missing. When he asked what happened to our piglets, we confessed that we had sold them. He immediately put us in the truck and drove us back to the farm where we had sold the little pigs. He returned the $1.50 to the farmer and drove us and the piglets back to the Home. Nothing else was said about our actions for at least a week, but then the Superintendent called us in and asked for an explanation.

We told him we really believed that the piglets were totally ours. Because we wanted to go to the fair, even though we had been restricted from going, we sold the piglets. He explained that giving them to us was a figure of speech and not a transfer of ownership. We were not free to sell them.

The piglets had paid our fare to the fair, and we too fared well as punishment was not administered to us this time.

I still have a flare for the fair, but these days I pay my own fare.

# *Prayer Is a Powerful Thing*

## Edwin Chase

The hot, sultry July afternoon lay like a humid blanket around those of us hoeing corn in the large field next to the baseball diamond. Gnats buzzed around our ears. Corn dust made every pore of our skin itch, and salty perspiration stung our eyes as it traveled down our faces and dripped from our noses. We felt like the Hebrew slaves in Egypt. We knew we needed someone like Moses to deliver us from our toil under a relentless sun.

Too hot to complain and too tired to hope any longer for relief, we continued the drudgery of working the cornfield. Just when we were sure there would be no end to our ordeal, we noticed a mere puff of a cloud in the western sky—a cloud that began to enlarge.

With this slight encouragement, several of us peeled our sweat-soaked T-shirts from our bodies and laid them on the ground as prayer rugs. We bowed down on our knees and chanted in unison: "Oh God of the rain, save us!" After chanting for several minutes, we saw the cloud become larger, which was all we needed to completely set aside our hoes to bow and pray in earnest. The growing cloud was our opportunity to escape an afternoon of digging the ground in the hot sun.

Presently, we heard what sounded like a distant rumble of thunder. We looked first at one another and then gazed in amazement at the sky, watching the clusters of clouds knit together into a menacing, greenish-blue thundercloud that grew darker with every passing minute.

Whatever was happening in the heavens was gaining tremendous momentum. We watched in awe and curiosity as a wall of gray, extending from the cloud to the ground, moved toward us across the pasture. Too enraptured to state anything more than the obvious, my brother asked, "Is that rain?"

"Hope so," I answered with an increasing feeling of excitement. In no time at all, the grayness was upon us. It was not rain. It was hail! We grabbed our hoes and used our T-shirts to protect our heads from the ice pellets. The hail was followed by extremely cold, pelting raindrops that fell with increasing intensity. Unexpectedly, a lightning bolt struck so close that it caused my hair to stand on end. With that prompting, I was running toward shelter propelled by a mixture of terror and sheer delight.

The strong wind that accompanied the storm caused the rain to come at us sideways as if it were breaking the very natural laws of gravity. When we arrived at the senior boys' cottage, we were all soaking wet. As the thunderstorm continued to unleash its fury, rain came down in blinding sheets, and ditches overflowed with what looked like liquefied red Georgia clay. This was obviously what was meant by "a gully washer."

Sheltered from the pounding hail and rescued from the furnace of the cornfield, I proclaimed my love for a raging storm. We all relished it, and congratulated ourselves on the effectiveness of our prayers. We spent the rest of the afternoon playing hide-and-seek with one another rather than with the weeds in the field. We had been delivered from the bondage of the cornfield; and the thunderstorm had been our Moses.

Sometimes when I hear someone say, "Be careful what you pray for...you might get it," I think of that day in the cornfield.

Circa 1954

# Chapter Four

# *When Having Fun is the Main Event*

Sunshine Special meant one thing: fun. Once inside Ragan's Park, children from the Home enjoyed swimming, flying down a giant sliding board, roller skating, a train ride and a picnic lunch that capped off a great day. This annual event was anticipated with great excitement and was never a disappointment.

The Georgia State Fair is probably as popular today as it was in the forties. A night at the fair was like going to a place of fascination where you could win a teddy bear, see things you never dreamed of, be dazzled by fire eaters, be terrified in a haunted house, and steal a kiss on the Ferris Wheel.

The Georgia State Fair and Sunshine Special were sponsored by the Exchange Club of Macon. As a matter of fact, Sunshine Special was a creation of the Macon Exchange Club and was so well received, it later became a national program.

For several years the Edwin Gould Foundation invited a limited number of children across Georgia to enjoy the foundation's camp in Windham, New York, and a camp in the Catskills Mountains. Several children from the Home participated in these camps each year.

But closer to home - week in and week out - going to the movies was a wonderful break from the monotony of school and the drudgery of chores. A movie theater in the early days of film allowed the children from the Home to step into another world, the world of silent films with Laurel and Hardy and Charlie Chaplin.

Circa 1988

## Having Fun in Our Own Yard

By the middle of the twentieth century there were the classic films such as *Gone with the Wind, Giant,* and *Rebel without a Cause* that stretched our imaginations and raised important issues. On other days we would laugh ourselves silly with the antics of Dean Martin and Jerry Lewis. The movies gave us something very tangible: every week we *always* had something to look forward to. And that made all the difference.

Special occasions such as going to the movies, the fair, Sunshine Special and the camps in New York always brought out the kid in everyone. They were fun. And for children fun is the elixir of life. These enjoyable times are remembered with appreciation in the pages that follow.

Circa 1978

**Children on a Camping Trip**

# Remember the "Can-Can"

## James Kent

Each year the boys and girls who had not been involved in any serious behavior problems for the year were allowed to attend the State Fair. We also could not have any current "x's" on the disciplinary board.

Generally, arrangements were made for the children from the Home to have a minimum number of free rides. The older boys and girls were also given a quarter to spend as they pleased. Don't forget that in the 30s a quarter went a long way.

As I recall, one of the fair's strongest attractions for the older boys – 15 and up – was the girly shows. In these venues, a group of girls did the "Can-Can" on stage and a male comic told a few off-color jokes. The only drawback was that you had to be 18 years old to buy a ticket. We all tried to buy tickets, but our high pitched voices usually gave us away.

This is where I was able to make a real contribution to the cause. It seems that I have always had a deep and gruff voice; therefore, I was "selected" to buy the tickets. When I asked for the four tickets at ten cents per ticket, the man in the booth asked my age. I replied in my deepest voice that we were all 18-years-old or older. Without looking up, he sold me the tickets!

I gave each boy his ticket and led the way up the steps. We presented our tickets and entered the show. The fourth boy, Alex Martin, fell behind and called out, "Wait for me!" in his high-pitched voice. His voice and small stature gave him away immediately. He was stopped, his ticket taken, his money refunded, and he was publicly escorted back down the steps.

The ticket taker looked for the three of us, but we were hidden by the crowd and stayed to see the show.

By today's standards it was not much of a show, and we were terribly disappointed. The girls danced the "Can-Can." They kicked high and flipped up their long skirts, but the long ruffled pantaloons revealed nothing. And we had already heard all the jokes.

This was a disappointment, especially in the 1930s when there was no Six-Flags. But through it, I learned an important lesson: people will say almost anything to earn a buck. If something sounds too good to be true, I don't get too excited. I just remember the "Can-Can."

## *Special Sunshine in Our Lives*

### Mary Alice Hughes Roth

Each year there were special people and outstanding days that made my heart beat faster. One of the special people that caused excitement was Henry Kaplan who, with his wife, put on the best birthday parties any of us had ever experienced. Each month throughout the year he would order a beautiful cake for the children having a birthday that month and a dozen other cakes for those attending.

The head table was set up and the candles were lit. The children, whose birthdays were being celebrated, blew out the many candles and opened special gifts while Mr. Kaplan sat at one end and Mrs. Kaplan sat at the other. After eating the cake and ice cream, there was a time for mind games and singing "Happy Birthday." We were always made to feel so important by this wonderful couple.

In February as Valentine's Day rolled around, we always looked forward to the party given to the older boys and girls by the Centenary Methodist Church youth group. The large basement in the Edwin Jay Gould Senior Girls' Cottage was beautifully decorated with hearts and streamers. We danced, played games, ate goodies, and those who wanted to, exchanged valentines. In the upper floor of the little boys' cottage, the younger children also had a party with many decorations and refreshments appropriate for their age.

Another group that contributed to our growth and enjoyment were the owners of the local movie theaters. Every Thursday afternoon after school the girls were treated to a movie of their choice, as approved by the matrons of the cottages. Every Friday the boys were offered the same treat, although maybe a different movie. We had many vicarious experiences and enjoyed many great cartoons along with keeping up with the news of the day.

As spring approached, we looked forward to going to the Macon Municipal Auditorium to laugh at the clowns and see the many tricks the dogs and animals performed during the Shrine Circus sponsored by the local Shriners. Each year the Shriners would raise money so the children from the many childrens' homes in Macon could see the circus.

Good Friday always meant an Easter Egg Hunt. As school ended we couldn't wait for everyone to get on the bus to get home. The ladies of Mulberry Street Methodist Church always had the eggs dyed many colors and hidden by the time we arrived so we would not know where to find them. The prize egg was a wooden egg painted gold with beautiful decorations and fifty cents hidden inside. Of course, everyone wanted that egg.

The year I found the golden egg up in a large hemlock tree, I didn't care if I found another egg the rest of the afternoon. The egg hunt was only the beginning of the wonderful time we had at Easter. Prior to Easter Sunday, each of us had been shopping for new clothes so we would have new outfits for Easter and later in the season. On Easter we always felt so pretty or handsome.

Summer meant only one thing and that was the SUNSHINE SPECIAL which was made possible by the Exchange Club of Macon! The Men's Bible Class at Mulberry Street Methodist Church assisted in this adventure. The men arrived around nine o'clock in their own personal cars to take all the children to Ragan's Park for the day. What a treat! As the cars arrived, we would decide which car we wanted to ride in by the type of car it was or the color. My first experience with California plums happened on one of these trips. I didn't think I had ever tasted anything so sweet. We stayed the entire day at the park. There were mirrors that made you look thin and mirrors that made you look short and squatty. Our faces never looked like ourselves, and we laughed so hard we couldn't go past them without making some kind of face. There were skating, swimming, and picnicking. We usually didn't go swimming because we had the large Olympic pool at the Home. Lunch was brought to the park, and we had long tables at which to sit and rest while we ate. By four o'clock, the men returned to pick up their weary charges.  Sometimes I think the men had as much fun as we did.

Circa 1955

**Charles Hall at Sunshine Special,**
**the 1950s Version of Six Flags Over Georgia**

This was the first event of its kind by the Exchange Club of Macon.  In a few years, Exchange Clubs all across America were sponsoring Sunshine Specials of their own.

In September, we were treated to the Ringling Brothers' Circus.  I'm not sure who sponsored us, but we always enjoyed the elephants, horses, high-wire acts and clowns under the big tent.

As the weather turned a little cooler, the Exchange Club was also at full speed working on the Macon Fair.  Usually on the last Wednesday afternoon of October, we attended the fair.  If Allen Sanders was not there, we had another exchange member escort our group to the different rides.  No matter what the weather was, we had a great time.  When it was time to go home, we were full of cotton candy and candy apples.  Many of us had cupid dolls and prizes we had won at the different games where skill was required. It didn't take us long to fall asleep that night.

Some years the Lion's Club invited a group of older children to their club to play bingo. It was the first time some of us had played the game, and we really enjoyed it. We won prizes at some of the games, and at other times we just played for fun. Anytime we had a chance to get out of work on Saturday, we enjoyed it.

Another experience some of us had was a trip to Atlanta to see the Cyclorama and to see the carvings on Stone Mountain. In the Cyclorama we saw the Battle of Atlanta that was painted on a large canvas. The figures were so small but looked so real. Seeing this truly magnificent painting was without a doubt the first time we really thought about the Civil War. An interesting thing we learned about the painting was that the weight of the paint on the canvas made it extremely difficult to hang.

After lunch at Grant Park, we loaded the buses to travel several miles to Stone Mountain. The carvings of the figures of the Confederate soldiers were not complete, but we didn't know that. When we pulled up to the area, all we saw was a small building where some maintenance workers had some equipment. Beside the building was a telescope for viewing the carvings which were impressive and very large. It wasn't until the late sixties that the carvings were completed, and a park was opened for people to visit with many rides and attractions.

In remembering events of the fifties, I'd like to thank those who brought sunshine into our lives, touched our lives, and gave us enjoyable things to do and to look forward to.

# "Lemonade ... and Sunshine Special"

## Zimmie Irwin Goings

Not all days in our lives stand out as highlights ... some are just routine ... but even on routine days and in mundane situations one can find something to smile about.

Oftentimes we older girls at the Methodist Home spent summer afternoons shelling beans on the front porch of the Gould Girls' Building ... shelling bushel basket after bushel basket and waiting for the boys to bring more. It was during that time that we sang songs together ... learned to harmonize ... sang the latest Hit Parade tunes. We talked about many things ... perhaps about the Macon Peaches baseball team ... perhaps the major leagues, too, and we knew as much as most kids about who batted in what ... who had the most home runs ... who was the favorite movie star ... favorite singer or what have you. We knew that once the beans were shelled, we could go to the pool. We never considered that to be routine ... rather a chance for another joyful time.

Woven into those days of summer were special times ... highlights of the summer, if you will ... days that will always remind us of sunshine and happiness.

One morning recently my thoughts turned to the previous day's lunch and some lemonade I'd enjoyed. I began to get that sensation below the ears that one does when thinking about something tart ... LIKE LEMONADE. It took me back many years to a morning each year when the Exchange Club in Macon gave us a special day. It was called "Sunshine Special." A parade of mostly convertible cars came to the Home, all decorated with colorful crepe paper streamers, and piled us in, and took us through town in parade fashion to Ragan's Park for a day of special activities. We got to do things that we didn't get to do every day ... hardly ever, in fact. We roller-skated to the loud music that one could expect to hear in roller rinks. We went boating on the lake and had wonderful food to eat … AND LEMONADE. Yes, real lemonade. Not that we didn't have lemonade … but these were *barrels* of lemonade … lemonade where many lemons floated around inside … not made from some mix in a can that most of today's children are used to.

Circa 1952

**Difficult decisions at Sunshine Special: "Do I want to go swimming, roller skating, or ride the bumper cars?"**

I can taste the lemonade to this day and I still get that funny sensation under my ears from the thoughts of drinking it. I still hear the roller rink music, and I feel the water lapping around the rowboats on the lake.

When day was done, we put our thoughts into our memory banks for another day ... another year ... or perhaps today when we wish for a cold glass of lemonade from a pitcher where real lemons are ... And we are thankful to the people who gave us those days of "Sunshine Special."

# A Dream Vacation in the Catskills

## Wallace Hubbard

I was especially privileged to enjoy a week's vacation at the Edwin Gould Foundation Camp at Windham, New York, and at a camp in the Catskills Mountains. My joy and excitement were exceeded only by the significance of being one of the ten children selected from several orphanages in South Georgia.

Circa 1933

**In the Catskills Edwin J. Gould provided a
wonderful camp experience for children.**

We boarded a train in Macon and traveled in a first-class "chair car" to Atlanta. There we boarded a Pullman car and slept overnight on the train before our arrival in New York. At camp there were activities of every kind, including swimming and hiking, all overseen by professional camp counselors. The week also included a trip to New York City for sightseeing and a trip to the Bronx Zoo. It was the first time that many of us had ever seen an escalator. But I especially remember the camp, the evening campfires, roasting marshmallows and listening to scary ghost stories, narrated by our camp counselor, a master story teller.

A good time was had by all. I have a memory I'll treasure forever.

# Chapter Five

# *Stellar Mischievous Pranks*

Think of all that must go into a magnificent prank. There must be forethought, creativity, good judgment (lest the prank go too far), a sense of humor and the courage to take a risk. These are not unworthy companions as we travel through life. They are assets. As youngsters, playing pranks was our way of practicing these important life skills. And who would not want to be identified with the antics of Tom Sawyer, Huckleberry Finn, and Andy Dufresne played by Tim Robbins in *Shawshank Redemption*?

From 1930 – 1960 there were several pranksters who lived at the Home and in this chapter we celebrate their splendid escapades. In the stories that follow we invite you to enter the world of some young pranksters preparing themselves for life.

**Circa 1956**

**Charles Hall Making a Face**

# The Phony Nickel Caper

## James Kent

Slot machines were very popular in the 1930s, as they are today in malls and game arcades. You insert a coin, and a crane with a claw-like device hovers over a toy and hopefully picks up the toy of your choice. Unfortunately, the claw rarely holds the toy long enough to drop it down the chute. Back then the machines were all mechanical, not electrical, and you worked the crane by hand. Either way you walked away feeling cheated. After many failures, we all felt cheated and wanted revenge.

We learned that the mechanical slot machines would work on any hard disk that was the same size and thickness of a nickel. The question was what did we have that could easily be turned into a phony nickel that would trip the lever and work the machine? First we tried pounding lead slugs into the required shape, but more often than not, they jammed the machine. Now what?

One day as we sat around breaking up old Victrola records, we realized that the record pieces could be easily transformed into "nickels." Using a file, it took a long time to make the phony "nickels."

When the fair arrived in town, we still did not have enough "nickels" to suit us. Still we were going to cheat the cheater as each one of us had several "nickels." We never expected to win a prize. We would have fun cheating the cheater, and it would not cost us a nickel! We chose a machine and put in our "nickels." To our complete joy, they worked. However, they did not make the loud clink that a real nickel made as it dropped into the pot. We were able to use only a couple of our "nickels" before being spotted and forced to run into the crowd. We proudly carried our "real nickels" home knowing that we had really cheated the cheater.

# *Ditch the Snacks*

## **James Kent**

When I was in my teens at the Home, the boys my age and I were always looking for something to eat. During the spring and summer, this was not a great problem because fresh vegetables such as tomatoes, sweet potatoes, corn, and Irish or white potatoes were plentiful. With a little ingenuity, we could cook almost anything in a gallon tin can. When finished, just add salt and pepper.

We cooked these vegetables using the steam from the boiler that supplied steam to the kitchen and laundry. We boys rigged up a valve that let the steam trickle through the water in the tin can. It also worked well for making boiled salty peanuts and any other food that could be cooked by boiling.

Muscadines, scuppernongs, fox grapes, plums, blackberries and other wild fruit and nuts, which grew in the nearby woods, made wonderful snacks in season. We also raided nearby melon patches and peach orchards. We were always careful not to destroy or harm the vines, trees, or unripe fruit. It seemed a little sinful at the time.

On one occasion, I recall a farmer coming out of his house shouting at us, firing his shotgun in the air, and having a good belly laugh as we fled for our lives. I once had the opportunity to hear the farmers tell their stories about scaring the daylights out of some boys. I believe they knew we were the culprits in their fields. They were careful to point out that their crops were never harmed in any way. It appeared that they were trying to protect us.

However, during the winter and early spring these snacks were not available to us. Therefore, we had to find other sources. We would carefully look through the peanut vine hay donated to the Home and collect the peanuts left on the vines. There were plenty of goodies in the kitchen, but it was always locked at night.

The girls who worked in the kitchen were free to take (or at least they freely took) snacks back to their cottages for themselves and the other girls. We boys had to be creative if we wanted to get at these snacks. The challenge was to get into a locked kitchen. On occasion, the doors were left unlocked. I am not sure if the doors were left open on purpose or by accident. Sometimes the girls would do us a favor and intentionally leave a door unlocked. This was infrequent though, and there were long dry spells. To overcome this, I began to experiment with opening locks without a key and/or making skeleton keys. I got rather good at it, and I taught others, so we could get into the kitchen anytime we wanted to have a snack at night.

The ability to get snacks at night was acquired the same year it was decided to put a new drain in for the hot water that supplied heat and hot water for the boys' cottages. This called for a ditch to be dug. During the digging process, a temporary bridge was built over it. When the ditch was completed, the bridge was removed.

After a particular day's hard work, we boys needed a nighttime snack. Four of the boys sneaked out, used one of the skeleton keys, got into the kitchen, gathered up our snacks and started to leave. Then a second group approached the kitchen. Upon hearing the approach of the second group, the first group decided it was time to make a hasty exit, fearing the farm manager was coming. We left running with our hands full of snacks. In our rush, we forgot that the bridge over the ditch had been removed.

It was not a pretty sight. The snacks were ditched as were four boys. Luckily, no one was hurt except for a few bruises and hard feelings.

About an hour later, we went back and had our midnight snack. It seems that teenage boys want to eat all the time!

**Editor's Note:** James Kent served with distinction in WWII. Enlisting as a PFC, he landed in Italy as a Lieutenant and at one time was missing and presumed dead until it was confirmed he was a POW. Later, James retired as a Lieutenant Colonel. As you read his stories, you will not be surprised that he learned his resourcefulness and resiliency as a boy at the Home, who delighted in an endless stream of mischievous yet harmless capers.

Circa 1954

**Pranks are designed to catch someone off guard.**

## *The Higher You Go, the Harder You Fall*

### Edwin Chase

Ever since boys first gathered in groups, I suppose, there has always been one who claimed he could do everything better than the rest. The Home was no exception. I distinctly recall one boy, a little older than I, who constantly boasted that he could sprint faster, jump higher, and generally run circles around us average guys – or so he claimed.

One Saturday afternoon, we were engaged in one of our favorite pastimes, jumping bicycles across a small gully. We would peddle as fast as possible. At the edge of a three-foot dip, we would jerk the handlebars up, remain airborne for a few seconds, and then land, hopefully on two wheels, and come to a safe stop. However, if one did not maneuver just right and crashed instead, landing could be a painful experience, especially on hard clay ground littered with small pebbles. A careless or unskilled gully-jumper could wind up with a severe case of "road rash."

Before long, our own established braggart, spouting how he could out jump all of us, began pointing out everything *we* were doing wrong. Tired of his big mouth and condescending attitude, some of the guys decided to take matters into their own hands. While some of the boys distracted our blustering self-proclaimed master of everything, another surreptitiously adjusted the front wheel of his untended bicycle. Gruffly telling us to make way because he was about to show us how it was supposed to be done, the boy mounted his now-modified bike. We waited expectantly as he flew across the lawn at an impressive speed, approached the gully, and jerked up on the handlebars. The bike soared into the air, a thing of beauty. Boy and bike were airborne. The only problem was that his front wheel was still earthbound, rolling freely by itself. I will never forget the look of shock, surprise, and terror in that boy's eyes. There were no broken bones, but he got the worst case of "road rash" I have ever seen. For a very long time, we "average guys" relished what came to be known as the Great Bicycle Caper.

Circa 1953

**One of the boys in this picture was in for a huge surprise!**

# *Keep Your Hair Dry*

## Edwin Chase

Those of us who attempted to sneak into the swimming pool late at night had to be proficient in a variety of athletic skills because the pool was located only yards from Superintendent Woodall's back porch. One thing was certain. If the matron in our cottage went to bed at 9:30 P.M., we were out the door by 10:00 P.M.

One night, several of us boys from the senior boys' cottage made our way in the dark through the park to the pool. Our first shadowy challenge completed, it was then necessary to scale a five-foot wire fence which surrounded the pool. Once over that hurdle, we strategically placed a bench against the fence to furnish a quick "leap and bound" get-away if needed. With the geographical logistics of our mission well executed, it was imperative to remind ourselves of the cardinal rule: *Do not get your hair wet!*

While enjoying the cool water and the deep satisfaction of just being there, the worst possible thing happened - Dr. Woodall's back porch light came on! Instantly, we were out of the water and over the fence in one bound, running barefooted at break-neck speed through the park's total darkness! Our intimate knowledge of the park came in handy, allowing us to traverse our way behind the laundry and up the hill to our cottage. "Duck the clothesline in the backyard!" someone in our group warned. But, it was too late. One of our companions was literally "clotheslined," which sent us all scampering haphazardly into our cottage as we stifled our laughter. Once inside, we fought to contain ourselves and tiptoed to our rooms where we dried quickly and got into our beds, trying our best not to breathe hard.

Settling into slumber, we knew that if anyone were to make a bed check searching for the nocturnal swimmers, all we had to do was look perplexed and present our dry heads as evidence of our innocence. But a stethoscope to the chest would have instantly given us away.

Circa 1955

**A refreshing dip in the pool at midnight was much more exciting than swimming in broad daylight.**

# *Sometimes Things Aren't What They Seem*

## Edwin Chase

When I was about ten years of age, the boys from the Methodist Children's Home passed out bulletins at the front door of the Vineville Methodist Church.  I guess it was the huge wooden doors and the massive columns of that Greek Revival structure that somehow made us feel like we were doing something really big.  One of the real ushers, a pleasant man in his early sixties, would frequently leave his post as a greeter in the narthex and conceal himself behind one of the huge columns of the church to sneak a puff from his cigar.  After lighting the cigar and taking a few puffs, the gentleman would carefully hide the still-burning stogie in a crevice.  He would then regularly sneak back to the same place and take another couple of puffs.

What fun I had moving his cigar from one hiding place and putting it in another.  Watching him search for his missing cigar was great.  He would scratch the back of his head, widen his eyes and put on a look of utter bewilderment as if to say, "Where did I put my cigar?"  Sure that his memory was failing, this fine man never caught on.  Sometimes things aren't what they seem.

The first time I was in the second grade a mystery was clarified by the simple act of learning to read.  At the top of our church bulletin was always the italicized sentence: "If you must waste, waste paper."  Young though I was, the statement made perfect sense to me:  Because there was so much paper in the world, it would be okay to waste it.  However, when I learned to read rather than guessing at words, I discovered a whole new meaning.  The weekly admonition on the church bulletin actually said, "If you must whisper, whisper a prayer."  That made a lot more sense.  Sometimes things aren't what they seem.

Absolutely the most forbidden sin was to fall asleep in church.  To get caught dozing during the sermon always meant extra chores on Sunday afternoon, the bane of a young boy's life. Our quest to remain alert was hindered by the thick Scottish brogue of Dr. King Vivian, a distinguished, erudite man who was not even understood by most adults in the congregation, who judged his sermons as "over their heads." Certainly as a second grader (who should have been in the fifth!) I had no chance of understanding him. So the other boys and I devised a scheme which would make the sermon time more interesting.

Along with his dialect, Dr. Vivian also carried with him several easily noticeable quirks and mannerisms. He would frequently take off his glasses, rub his chin, place his hands behind his back, or spread his hands across the pulpit Bible. We had every move categorized and listed. Each Sunday, before we arrived at church, we organizers would give each "boy-turned-contestant" a scorecard of Dr. Vivian's habitual gestures. One of us was selected to be the official scorekeeper. With each contestant contributing a quarter to the game, we were ready to tally the preacher's mannerisms during the sermon and then compare them to the official score keeper's count. The boy with the score closest to the official tally won the jackpot and stood to walk away with $2.00! Big money back then. However, our game had an unexpected result. Some worshipers began to notice our rapt attention during the sermon. One woman said to another, "Those boys from the Home really listen to the preacher."

"Listen, nothing," said another woman, "They take notes!"

Sometimes, things just aren't what they seem.

When I was in the eighth grade, the Cherokee Heights Methodist Church in Macon sponsored a dance on Saturday nights to keep the teenagers off the streets. It was almost too successful. Every teenager and juvenile delinquent, who was not in jail, was at Cherokee Heights on Saturday night. The small fellowship hall was packed each week as we danced to our favorite records, *In the Still of the Night* and Elvis' second big hit, *Don't Be Cruel*. The aroma of those dances was unforgettable, a combination of *Touche-Moi* and *Clearasil*. The dress in the late fifties was blue jeans, a white T-shirt and an orlon sweater.

However, the really tough guys could not be missed because they wore black leather jackets with their hair combed in ducktails with lots of "grease." Hence, the movie by the same name. However, not all the guys who donned black leather were tough guys. In fact, Buddy Ferguson, who had sold me his Gibson guitar, was a respected tenth grader even though his attire was identical to the motorcycle guys.

During one Saturday dance, Buddy had greeted me as I entered. Later, when I saw his familiar black jacket in front of me, I remembered I had to tell him something. So, I grabbed him by the shoulder and said, "Hey, Buddy." With lightening speed, the fellow in the black jacket whirled around and grabbed me by my sweater. He picked me up and pushed my back against the wall. He held me up in the air against the wall with one hand while his other formed a gigantic fist. I could feel the blood draining from my face and wondered how many teeth would be missing when this was over. The fellow glaring at me was obviously not Buddy Ferguson. It was one of the most feared boys in the county. This fellow was seventeen years old and weighed 180 pounds, and was known for his ability as a street fighter.

"What do you want!?!" he growled.

When I could catch my breath, I stammered, "I thought you were B-B-Buddy Ferguson." Out of the corner of my eye I could see Rosemary Lawson looking up at me in stark terror.

After what seemed an eternity, he said, "Don't ever touch me again!" And he lowered me to the floor. My medium size orlon sweater was now extra large. On wobbly legs and fighting back a wave of nausea, I made my way out into the fresh air, grateful to be in one piece. I was amazed at how quickly I had stepped into harm's way. Sometimes things aren't what they seem.

# Chapter Six

## *The Wonder and Excitement of Saint Simons Island*

For many children their week-long visit to St. Simons Island was their first extended visit at the beach. For some it was their first time to see the ocean. They were at first astonished then captivated by the expansive horizon that glistened in the sun. And the white beach seemed to stretch forever.

The children and staff stayed at Camp Marion, an old two story wooden structure with broad screened-in porches. There was a huge yard with live oak trees and Spanish moss. This vacation spot was located less than a mile from the Coast Guard Station.

Circa 1978

**Lighthouse at Saint Simons**

The trip to St. Simons was less than glamorous. The children were driven in an old un-air-conditioned yellow school bus equipped with a manual transmission that usually grinded its way into fourth gear. The young vacationers traveled state roads and the trip would take the better part of a day.

However, the excitement of the children made up for any discomfort. They were headed to the beach! The stories in this chapter give a glimpse of life on St. Simons through the wistful eyes of youth.

Circa 1952

**Jossie Walker Playing the Ukulele at Saint Simons Island**

## *Summer's Passing...and...*
## *The Ocean in a Seashell and A Place Called Saint Simons*

### Zimmie Irwin Goings

Circa 1952

**Seated atop the post is the author of this story, someone who has written several books of her own.**

## Summer's Passing

I find myself missing summer as it passes.  Each August I do, for often in summer we add experiences to our lives that provide happy thoughts for later years.   Happy thoughts ... perhaps sensitive thoughts ... that will fill our memory banks for a later time when we look to that time to remember ... to sustain us ... perhaps because one summer we couldn't make a memory but rather needed to relive one.  At least that is how it seems to me ... as summer passes.

## The Ocean in a Seashell ... and A Place Called St. Simons

I suppose I was about thirteen-years old and only then was I about to discover the ocean and its wonders ... on an island called St. Simons ... and a place called Camp Marion ... somewhere off the coast of Georgia.

Do you remember the first time you saw the ocean ... listened to its mood ... felt its strength ... watched the waves break on the sand and then gently, it seems, return to sea?  Do you remember the first time you held a seashell to your ear and listened to the ocean in it?  And you thought, "How could that be?"  How can one capture the sound of the sea in a seashell?  I don't yet know.

Do you remember seeing gray clouds above the ocean and thinking how much alike they and the ocean seemed ... both showing their "anger" ... one giving a message to the other?  But do you also remember the ocean under a sunny summer sky ... sunshine that you wanted to bask in all day ... the lazy feel of the day, except for gleeful children ... how the waves seemed still to exert their strength and forcefulness, but taking on a relaxing and playful way sometimes?

Do you remember the first time you saw the ocean lit by the moon ... and felt the cool sand on the shore beneath your feet ... sort of moving beneath your toes as the water would come in and then take the sand from beneath your toes as it washed back out to sea?  I suppose it's the moon that controls all this going and coming. Do you remember the first time someone showed you the lights in moonlit water ... the phosphorous that gleams in the water at night? And do you remember the little fiddler crabs that raced along the shore at night in their sideways manner and you just knew that you were going to step on one? Do you remember the first time you saw a jellyfish and discovered how quickly you could move to get away from it?

Do you remember feeling the sea breeze in your hair ... and how it brought a bit of a chill to your sunburned body?

Some of us still do ... I'm sure of it!

It was afternoon when we children from the Home got our first glimpse of God's ocean in all its immenseness ... and heard the sounds of the crashing waves ... learned to respect the water that He has given us to enjoy and to learn from. It was a gray afternoon as I recall ... but somehow we could not have been brought so far to see this wonder and have to wait. We learned that though the waves come in to meet you ... the spirit that lives beneath them ... the tide ... wants to carry you somewhere else, and one must be careful. We learned caution that first day and were watched over lest something should happen to one of us.

We were the children from the Methodist Children's Home ... given a chance for a vacation close to the seashore on St. Simons Island. We enjoyed our days in the sun as perhaps other children might not. It seems we walked to the beach each morning after breakfast and chores, and then again sometimes in the afternoon if there were no other plans. It was a nice walk ... with a lot of talking and laughing ... walking gingerly across the hot sand so as not to scorch our feet ... and gingerly so as not to get sandspurs in our feet ... and as I believe I remember, so as not to stir up ant hills. Yes, the sand was so hot that the only known way to save our feet was to hop from one patch of grass to another ... barefoot as Southern children would be.

We passed by the Coast Guard Station and played in its shadow during the hours that flew by too quickly... hearing the lapping of the waves at water's edge. I remember looking far down the beach where a large hotel with terra cotta roof tiles stood gleaming in the sun and learning at some point that it was The

King and Prince Hotel. I promised myself that one day when I was grown, I would stay there ... where the people now stayed who must have "lots of money." I'm a believer in promises kept, and so mine was. And from the King and Prince Hotel I could now look down the beach toward where we must have played long ago ... and wondered exactly where.

It was exciting to get on the Home's bus and ride along the roads of St. Simons in the evening ... to see the moon shining ... to hear the cicadas or tree frogs or crickets or katydids or whatever were all the night sounds. It was splendid to go into the village of St. Simons and shop in the little stores ... and there we learned about "Snowballs."

I suppose it was then and there that most of us first learned about lighthouses and their importance ... that they and their keepers are responsible for those out at sea ... a message to the sailors and seafarers and one form of light to bring them safely to shore. Christ is the other.

We learned the early history of the island and its settlers ... the early days of Methodism in this country ... about John and Charles Wesley ... though their Christ Church later built by Anson Dodge embraces an Episcopal faith. Of course, we have been related over the years .... the Methodists and the Episcopalians. We learned about the wars fought on and about the island ... walked through the grounds of Fort Frederica which still reminds one today of those times. We became used to the marshes that are so much a part of the island's unique topography.

Though on vacation, Sunday mornings took us to a church in the community, and we sang songs and read readings just as if at home.

There are so many thoughts of Camp Marion and the island ... the screened porches where we slept in bunk beds ... the sulfur in the water ... the smell of it in the air ... the cold water in the shower house out back ...I suppose some of us .... and I for one ... shed a few tears when our time was over on St. Simons each year ... for we had seen wonders ... bonded even more closely with one another ... and knew that this was a time like none other ... our first sight of the sea ... the sand ... the sounds of the sea in the seashell ... the riplets of the sea at water's edge teasing our young feet ... the walking creatures called crabs ... that young boys like to chase young girls with to make them run and squeal with fright ... the seabirds that flew about overhead and searched the sea below with their sharp eyes for their daily nourishment. We had suntanned bodies ... a few more freckles here and there ... images engraved in our memories ... and stories to tell ... yes, stories to tell ... even today ... as summer passes.

# A Joyous Week at the Beach

### Edwin Chase

As a twelve-year old on the beaches of St. Simons Island, I was enthralled as much as John Wesley had been appalled. Brother Wesley complained about the deer flies, the sand gnats, and the oppressive heat. But for me, Camp Marion at St. Simons Island was a place of wonder and enchantment.

Several weeks prior to our trip to the beach it had rained excessively. As we drove along country roads in our yellow school bus, I noticed that water had filled the ditches on both sides of the road most of the way to St. Simons. Cloudy skies had darkened our days for weeks, and I longed for a glimpse of the sun. With my eyes fixed on the clouds hoping for a patch of blue, I prayed for sunshine all the way to St. Simons. By the time we arrived, gray skies had given way to blue, and the warm sun was tempered by a gentle sea breeze. It was going to be a great week!

Camp Marion was unique in and of itself. There were live oak trees in the backyard that you didn't have to climb. You could walk into and up the tree without having to work very much. It was as though the tree invited you into its branches. One limb was so low to the ground and so huge that as a child you could stand on the limb and literally walk up the branch into the tree. Such hospitable trees did not exist in Macon.

In the open area downstairs at Camp Marion was a place where we could play checkers and other board games. The food at Camp Marion was a double-edged sword. On the positive side, there were fish fries that I savored, and for the first time I ate boiled shrimp until I thought I would certainly turn into one. But breakfast was unusually horrid. Back in the early fifties the sulfur water of St. Simons tasted like rotten eggs. For breakfast in the morning, this water was mixed with Carnation Evaporated Milk and chilled. I was told that the milk came from a sea cow. I vowed on the spot that if I ever saw a sea cow, I would kill it.

I later learned that there were such things as sea cows, but they didn't produce this awful breakfast beverage. We usually went to the beach twice a day, and for safety's sake we had a buddy system. When a whistle blew, we had to hold our buddy's hand up. Playing in the surf and making sand castles, we did all the wonderful things that children do at the beach.

But one particular experience was unforgettable. James Joyce in his book, *Portrait of an Artist as a Young Man,* tells of his concrete thinking style as a young man. Things that were cold and wet he disliked. He much preferred things that were dry and warm. Then at age fourteen he was kissed by a girl. The kiss was warm and moist, which totally confused Mr. Joyce.

As a young man, I had a similar experience. While swimming in the ocean one afternoon, letting the waves lift us off our feet and gently set us down again, a school of jellyfish came into our area unnoticed. One after another several boys doubled over in pain. The tentacles of the jellyfish had brushed the sides of our legs leaving their stingers on the surface of our skin. We ran to the beach, and someone suggested that we pack our legs in wet mud, which we did as fast as we could. It didn't take long to discover that "solution" was totally ineffective. In agony, we grabbed our towels and began to run back to Camp Marion. Maybe there was some relief to be found there.

We raced into the building and, while dancing around in pain, described our dilemma to several teenage girls who wanted to help, but did not know what to do. Finally, someone suggested rubbing our legs with Witch Hazel, a kind of mild antiseptic. I was willing to try *anything*. The stinging sensation caused by the active stinging cells of the jellyfish was unbearable. We were told to lie down on the tables while the girls rubbed the Witch Hazel on our thighs and calves. The cure worked temporarily. I was totally distracted and a little confused. How could something be so painful and so wonderful at the same time! After a while, the stinging cells died, and the pain subsided.

Circa 1952

**The sand between your toes and a gentle sea breeze
make the beach unforgettable.**

Camp Marion for me was a place of stark contrasts. The
week went from dreary rain to sparkling sunshine – from Georgia

clay to white sand, and from pine trees that say "Climb me if you can," to live oaks that say, "Please climb me, enjoy my branches." The everyday chores of running a dairy farm gave way to a week of carefree activities. The pain of the jellyfish stood in stark contrast to the attention of the young girls. Finally, the pure wholesome milk from our dairy contrasted with the hideous milk served at Camp Marion. But the positive aspects of a magical week at the beach far outshone the negatives.

# *Camp Marion on My Mind*

**Mary Alice Hughes Roth**

Driving by the King and Prince Hotel on Saint Simon's Island recently brought back memories of Camp Marion which was located near there in the forties and fifties. The two-storied white building with its screened-in porches sat majestically among the giant live oak trees with the hanging, gray Spanish moss waving softly in the June breezes. The camp didn't realize it was sitting on such valuable property just a few doors from the King and Prince Hotel until it was torn down for more elite housing.

The second week of June brought such excitement and joy to eagerly awaiting boys and girls who had been preparing for the journey to the coast since school ended for the summer. The shorts had been washed and pressed, the bathing suits had been tried on a dozen times to make sure they fit, and the shoes were tucked neatly in each suitcase.

On the Monday morning of the departure, no one wanted much for breakfast, and everyone made sure that his or her toothbrush was packed. The food for the week was the first to be loaded and then the luggage. No one had to be told twice to get on the yellow school bus with "Methodist Children's Home" written on the sides just under the windows. Soon each window was lowered and every seat found. Those not going until the following week waved good-bye, and off we went.

Lunch was always a special treat since we were treated by the Baxley Methodist Church that was located little more than halfway to the camp. Along the way we also saw flags displayed and learned there was a day called "Flag Day" on June 14.

As the bus rumbled along, we knew we were getting closer to the camp when the smell of sulfur water and marsh grass permeated the air. Those who had been before remembered how awful the water tasted compared to Macon's good water. We were told that sulfur water loses its bad taste if it is put in the refrigerator. Don't believe it!

All eyes were eagerly watching for the sight of the camp. Once we were stopped, it didn't take long for the quietness to be broken with directions given, luggage claimed, and beds scooped up. Just sleeping on bunk beds was excitement enough. The older boys were part of the unloading crew, and they usually were assigned the beds on the screened-in porches. As usual each person claimed his/her territory and soon became comfortable for the week.

The cooks, Josie and Sally, didn't take long finding the right ingredients for the evening meal. As the aroma of supper cooking lifted into the air, our shoes were off, and it wasn't long before our feet were black from the sand around the camp. At no time had sand felt as good between the toes as it did while we ate ice cream sandwiches and chased after one another.

At supper we sat at long tables with attached benches, and most of the time we picked up our plates from the kitchen when it was time to eat. As usual a clean up crew was assigned, and before long we were running around again until it was time for showers and bed.

It was always a chore for the person who slept closest to the light switch because someone always forgot something or had to go to the bathroom "one more time." Before bed each night, we always had our nightly devotionals to help us rest better and to be closer to God. That first night no one had trouble going to sleep, but later as the week wore on we were eager to hear each morning who had found sandspurs in their bed or who had discovered their bed short-sheeted.

As the sun rose over the marshes each day, the camp was abuzz with morning chores and breakfast. Since being told that sea cows and sea horses were in the ocean, which we really didn't believe, we were eager to get to the beach and see for the first time what the ocean really looked like. By mid-morning we set off barefooted to the beach. The bits of broken seashells were sharp, but we quickly learned to walk around them. The water was cool, and the breeze in our faces felt wonderful. We could have stayed for hours, but by eleven-thirty we were on our way back to camp. As we started out everything was fine except for a few sandspurs until we hit the sand behind the dunes. Our tender feet had never encountered such blistering heat. Soon, instead of walking, we were hip-hopping or running to get to grass patches. After a couple of days, we were prepared for each trip back.

Circa 1952

**Camp Marion was a great place to climb trees,
play and pose with new friends.**

Lunch each day was wonderful since the time at the beach always left us famished. Just as back at home we always had a good hot meal, and afterwards, as usual, we always had to have "quiet hour" until mid-afternoon. That not only made us bearable for the rest of the day, it also gave the adults time for themselves.

As soon as "quiet hour" was over, we hit the trees outside. The low hanging branches of the live oaks were excellent for climbing or walking on. You could actually climb onto a low hanging branch and climb into the tree without ever touching the tree trunk! We spent more energy during that week doing things so simple, yet so wonderful to a growing child. Each afternoon our snack was watermelon, cookies or ice cream; but, no matter what, it was *good.*

The shrimp served one night at the camp was also a special treat because most of us had never eaten shrimp and didn't know what to do with the little critters. Most of the time the shrimp were fried and delicious! Occasionally we were treated to ice cream in town by one of the "former boys from the Home" who lived in Brunswick.

As the week flew by, we couldn't believe it was time to go home on Saturday. We were tanned, happy, and eager to tell the others back home all that we had done. I know each of us had grown a couple of inches by the time we left. The last visit to the beach was extra special even if we hadn't seen a single sea cow. It was not until later that I learned the there is a sea cow called a "Manatee."

No matter how many wonderful experiences I may have, none will take the place of Camp Marion.

Circa 1998

# Chapter Seven

## *Reflections on a Childhood Restored*

The significance of any event is revealed only upon reflection. The word, *reflect,* comes from two Latin words that mean "to bend back" like looking over your shoulder at something you saw at a glance.

Circa 1987

**There are times when you just have to stop and think.**

Circa 1972

**"Can you believe, we had a real astronaut visit us yesterday?"**
**(Astronaut Sonny Carter actually did.)**

Circa 1976

**Ready or not, sometimes you just have to hug someone.**

When we reflect on our childhoods, we always have a choice: we can reflect in the spirit of thanksgiving or resentment. The stories in this chapter were written by adults who have chosen to reflect with gratitude on a childhood they would not have chosen. Yet upon reflection they saw God's hand upon their lives and the sacredness of their stories – and chose to share them.

# *Beginnings...The Main Building*

### Zimmie Irwin Goings

Beginnings vary from one child to another.  Circumstances are different ... places of beginning are different ... families are different ... disciplines different ...the blendings of which partly make us who we are.

I always feel like a part of my life has been put back together to talk with someone today about the Methodist Children's Home where my childhood from the age of six and on ... was spent.

I've often been asked about my parents ... sometimes questions that carried with them the assumption that perhaps they abandoned me or "gave me up" ... or that perhaps they were residents of "Milledgeville," a mental hospital in the State of Georgia, and I would answer, "No, my mother was simply sick. She died when I was five years old, from complications of surgery ... a blood clot that went to her heart following surgery.  My father died sometime later after I went to live at the Home.  No, my parents were both mentally and psychologically sound; it was just 'the times' that didn't offer the same good medical practices that we have today."

When I'm asked about "old wounds," I tell them: "I don't believe that I have any old wounds."  I and many others were children of circumstances ... circumstances that we bore no responsibility for.  Rather, we lived together as a family of friends ... but a family nevertheless ... caring for one another ... laughing ... sometimes crying ... learning ... and "holding one another up" as we went along.  There were those who were perhaps embarrassed to live in the children's home because we were singled out as "home children" ... but then there were those in Macon who were called "mill children."  They may have been less well off than we.  And then there were "the city children."  We were privileged in ways that others may not have been ... and we were not privileged in ways that others were.

My childhood friend, Jossie, and I talk from time to time about these things and those people who always had a touch of pity in their voices when they realized we were "from the Home." We'd say to them in a gentle but laughing way, "Oh, that's okay; we turned out 'almost normal.'" We turned out just absolutely normal and we are strong ... sensitive ... and fun-loving people ... even sixty or so years later.

And, yes, I might say, I miss having had parents as I grew up ... but no, I don't harbor bitterness or feel wounded. Wounds are more apt to be those hurts of abandoned children ... abused children ... and the like. I was simply orphaned. Perhaps the way we lived at the Home ... looking to the others there ... as they did to me ... gave us strength .... taught us closeness ... loyalty to friends ... the desire to help one another ... to be kind and to treat one another as one would want to be treated.

I never want to come across as having been a poor, pitiful child, but rather one who survived because of her inner spirit. It is that which carries one through trials ... and helps one to grow and love. I guess I treat gently and softly and mostly with a clear objective mind our lives at the Home. Things were not always easy ... often were not easy ... but our spirits carried us.

I always hope for light to be shed on the strength of children who came to the Home to live and went along in their lives ... strong and better than they may have been ... but, not "poor, pitiful." There is so much to see in the hearts and souls of those who have shared lives at the Home.

There are a million little stories that the children could and can tell ... but these are the feelings I have about myself as a child of the Home. I will never say that all was perfect there. There were disciplines then too harsh for the mistake ... not enough of the words "I love you" or "you're a special child" ... the positive strokes that have been encouraged at the Home in years since. There was a lot of emphasis on doing everything right ... small tolerance for less. But! There were enough of us to play almost any game. We became somewhat accomplished swimmers ...

were expected to do well in school.  We received good educations
... formal education ... and religious education ... were taught
music ... We enjoyed camp on St.  Simons Island and shared in
many activities that outside children enjoyed.  We had good food
and clothing ... warm beds ... and a beautiful environment ... and
most of all, one another.

We all had chores ... didn't we have chores??  Our still-
warm morning beds were made up before we walked away from
them ... before we could wipe the sleep from our eyes.  We ironed
clothes  as soon as we could reach the ironing board ... and
washed the tall windows in The Main Building with Bon Ami ...
often standing on the outside of the second – or third – story
window sills wiping windows with one hand and hanging on with
the other.

Circa 1955

**The Main Building with its expansive front porch was
a natural place to sit in a rocking chair and reflect.**

Our debates ... to say "squabbles" would be exaggerating ...
were never over larger things than whether we'd rather hear Frank
Sinatra sing or Bing Crosby ... Eddie Arnold or Ernest Tubb ...

whether we preferred Joe Dimaggio or some other player. Our competitiveness was generally in the swimming pool or in yard games. All in fun.

The Home is a lot different now ... in many good ways ... than when we were there, but many of us who were children at the Home in the 1940s and 1950s cling to thoughts of that special time.

# *Why Come Home?*

**James Kent**

As a boy growing up at the Home, I thought Homecoming was a huge event. Just prior to Homecoming, we would have several days of not working in the fields but preparing for the BIG DAY. On Homecoming Day, there would be an extra-special meal. Barbeque and Brunswick stew were not part of our daily fare. The older boys would spend all night barbequing whole hogs for this meal.

During the day, we had the opportunity to mix and mingle with boys and girls (and sometimes men and women) who formerly lived at the Home. They all had a tale of some sort as to what happened to them while they were there. The tales about the outside were taller, I suppose because our lives were, to a degree, isolated. However, the main event of the day was the baseball game between the current boys and the former boys. Most of the time, the Home boys won.

Now as a former resident of the Home, why do I always come back?

When I first joined the Army, I came back because I had no other home. The Home was the only home that I really knew. Also, many of the boys I left behind I considered good friends, almost blood brothers. We were that close. Of course, there were the girls. Most of the girls I knew were still there, and they were a definite attraction. As a matter of fact, they were the only girls I knew. Donna Kate Futch was the closest to being a sweetheart, but she left shortly after I went into the Army. I cannot honestly say that I had a sweetheart during those days.

However, there were several girls that I could and probably would have formed a relationship with under different conditions. There were Inez, Audrey, Norma, LaVern, Gloria, Wendy, and Annie Ruth just to mention a few. I thought they were all very pretty, nice, and friendly. However, this was not thought of as a drawing card because in the first few months of Army life, I met and dated some girls near Fort Bragg, North Carolina.

Most of my Army leave time was used to visit my sister. It was on one of these visits that I met the girl who was to become my wife. This does not explain why I like to visit the Home, but it does show why the visits became fewer and farther between. Of course, being in the Army with a limited amount of leave time and matching leave time with Homecoming was difficult. However, after retirement, I tried to make Homecoming every year. This goal was not always accomplished, but I tried.

Why do I come back? There was always the renewing of friendships. The few days I could spend with my brother, Wiley, and my sister, Georgia, were also strong drawing cards. Looking at the changes made on the campus and the new methods of handling the needs and wants of the children was most interesting. There is no doubt that the children today have it much easier with more opportunities than the children of my day.

I return at every opportunity because the Home was and is HOME TO ME!

# *What Goes Around, Comes Around*

## Bill Chase

One summer's day in Kingsport, Tennessee, my wife and I observed our son, Mark, cutting our front lawn grass. Joann commented, "You know, he hates cutting grass."

I replied, "Yes, I don't like it either, but it has to be done. Although Mark hates cutting grass, he does a good job of it. Where did he learn that?"

"Thankfully, he learned that from you," was Jo's response. My eyes glazed and memories stirred.

As a teenager at the Methodist Children's Home in Macon, Georgia, in the 1950s, I was among the boys that mowed the lawn, raked the leaves, milked the cows, and did the multitude of farm chores that had to be done. We didn't like the chores, but it was ingrained into each of us that we had to do them; they were our responsibilities.

I remembered cutting grass with a push mower. You used two hands to push the single-handle, which was attached to two wheels, which turned spiral shaped cutting blades mounted between the two wheels. Grass cutting became much easier and faster with the arrival of the gasoline powered mowers, but you still had to push them because mowers with power to the wheels were still not widely available. We liked the powered mowers; however, Mr. Durden, the Superintendent, didn't like it when, with one of them, I accidentally mowed down one of his prized camellia bushes.

I remembered "team raking" the leaves on the huge lawn in front of the Main Building. We created this way of raking. Instead of the usual way of each boy raking his individual square of turf, David suggested that we work together. He continued raking his line of leaves into my line of leaves, and suggested that I go over into his area and rake the newly-formed, longer line of leaves further down slope.

When Buddy, who was raking the area on the other side of me, saw what we were doing, he raked his leaves into the line as well. Other boys joined the process, and soon we had ten boys spread out across the huge lawn, all working together on consecutively formed lines of leaves. Raking leaves had become fun!

We learned a valuable lesson: you can find a little joy in an unpleasant circumstance. This notion served us well for the rest of our lives. When we finished a job and did it well, we were rewarded with the best joy of all – time for ourselves, ball games, swimming and other playful capers.

So the next time you are faced with a task you don't want to do, plunge into it anyway. Look for the little joys that are there; and even if you don't think you found a little fun, remember the satisfying joy of a job well done. As teenagers, we learned these things, and years later so did my son, Mark.

## *Sometimes Love Means Letting Go*

**Rene Lanier**

The story I wish to tell is as clear today as it was in 1949. This event broadened and deepened my love for life. It added to my understanding of the Creator's great wisdom and providence.

In the year of 1947, as newlyweds, my wife and I moved to Decatur, Georgia, to work at the Methodist Children's Home. Approximately seven months later, we had the opportunity to transfer to the Methodist Home in Macon, Georgia. I became the farm manager of the Home's farm. Because I love farm life and children, it was a dream job for me. Between February of 1948 and June of 1958, I had the opportunity to help the many children who were entrusted into our care.

An unforgettable event unfolded on a beautiful day in the late spring of 1949. As I recall, I was working in the vegetable garden not far from Pierce Avenue. When I looked up from the garden, I could see two small boys and a lady walking hand in hand, one on her right and one on her left. Later, I learned this was a mother bringing her two sons to the Home.

She and the boys had ridden the city bus to the corner of Vineville and Pierce. As they came closer into view, something made me stop my work and watch the threesome.

The boys appeared to be about the size to make them ready for the third and first grades. They were swinging their arms and talking to each other, as pride radiated from the mother's face. I thought at the time, "I hope my newly born son, Randy, would someday like to walk beside me – holding my hand, talking to me, with pride beaming from father to son." I mentally filed away the scene of a happy, contented family and returned to the work at hand.

Little did I know at that time, in just one hour, I would see the same mother walking that same path with tears flowing from her eyes and the sadness in her heart radiating through her whole being. She had left her two young sons in the care of the Methodist Home. What a tremendous sacrifice the mother had made. I could not imagine how difficult that act must have been for her that day.

However, about ten years later, I had the opportunity and privilege to sit with this mother at the high school graduation of her older son. As I watched her son being handed his diploma with honors, I've never experienced seeing any more pride and joy filling a person than I did that night. She told me, with tears streaming down her cheeks, how difficult it had been to leave her two sons in the care of someone else – strangers to her.

Many days and nights she wondered if she had made the right decision. That night, there was no doubt. The Methodist Home had given her sons the opportunity to better themselves and their future families. She thanked me, Mr. Woodall, and the entire staff for helping her sons become men.

The joy and pride that had seemed so evident to me that day ten years before – was back on this mother's face. Her heart was surely singing that night. I was unable to witness the younger son's graduation several years later as I had moved to Dalton. I am sure she again experienced the same joy and pride. This mother was later to experience what many only dream of – seeing both of her sons graduate from Emory University and move on to successful lives.

I am thankful that she made the sacrifice that day. I came to know and love two fine men. Her act of devotion helped keep her sons out of harm's way and opened many doors of opportunity for them. It has been my prayer that she continued to believe her sacrifice was the best possible course of action.

This story from my past is just one of many I could recount. Each and every child whom God has allowed to cross my life's path has such a story. Much happiness, pride, and joy comes to my family and me when a memory of a child is recalled or an accomplishment is celebrated. Their names, their faces, their lives have truly blessed my life.

I wish I could spend more time with each one of them. When my Heavenly Father calls me home, I look forward to singing His praises in the company of all my children.

# Ragged Robins…June Bugs and Bare Feet

## Zimmie Irwin Goings

Do you remember in your younger days when school was going to be out, what you looked forward to? What the summer brought? Some of those things come to my mind as though they happened just yesterday.

I remember going barefoot and how hot the days were, how the ground scorched our feet, and how we jumped from one patch of grass to another to keep from burning the soles of our feet…and, of course, not wanting to put on shoes. After all it was summer, and bare feet were like a bit of freedom. And still are.

I remember on the last day of school waiting in line to get typhoid shots…and nursing our arms for hours after.

Circa 1953

**A Leisurely Summer Afternoon with Friends and Bare Feet**

I remember sitting in a flower garden in the morning with other children where the sun shone gently…where "ragged robins" grew (bachelor buttons, you may call them) and listening to a storyteller recount wondrous stories to us. I favor that flower today...and cherish the moments.

I remember playing Hide 'n Seek in the twilight of the evening...and hiding behind the big oak trees hoping not to be found...at least until it got real dark...and then *hoping* to be found.

I remember watermelon cuttings and spitting watermelon seeds, Vacation Bible School and how we loved it, swimming...swimming...and swimming...and dragonflies.

I remember a missionary named Mary Culler White who visited us and told us about life in China and how the girls had their feet bound as children to keep their feet small. I still can see her expressive face and white hair.

I remember during the summer after graduation spending many hours reading Emily Post's ***Book of Etiquette***...hoping to be all that I should be as a young woman...thinking one day I might need to know about all those knives, forks and spoons...and white gloves up to the elbow with little buttons...and manners. Yes, manners!

And, I remember looking forward to going off for the first long time...to college and a strengthening of the foundation of my life.

I think of children...for I lived as one of a hundred...where there was always someone to do something with. I think of the awe that lived within us then and the awe that I recognize in children today.

And, yes, I think of "June Bugs," too. I should perhaps not tell you how we used to tie a string around one of their legs and let them fly...but we were children then...and certainly many Junes have come and gone since then. And, oh, yes, lightning bugs in a jar! Did you ever rub lightning bugs on your clothes...so that you could glow in the dark? Has any of that changed? I hope much of it never will.

# *Excerpts from Christmas Letters*

## Zimmie Irwin Goings

### Christmas and Chocolate Covered Cherries

I shall give a gift of chocolate covered cherries to my childhood friend for Christmas this year. It will be in a shoebox filled with other little things to remind us of our Christmases together in a Methodist Children's Home in South Georgia. We always got shoeboxes on Christmas morning...filled with nuts, oranges, tangerines, and, if we were lucky, a tall, fat candy cane and perhaps a couple of gifts outside the shoebox. We were happy...for we knew about the real Christmas. We donned chenille robes, wrapped towels on our heads, or put on wings, and pretended to be Mary, Joseph or the Angels at the Manger...even as children do today. The chocolate covered cherries are a reminder of a Sunday School teacher who gifted us with them for reading the Bible and learning I Corinthians 13...the book of love.

### Christmas Angels...Then and Now

I sat in the middle of the floor wrapping gifts the other night for a child sponsored by the Salvation Army Angel Program. I know not what she looks like...only that her name is Stephanie, her age is 9, and her size is 10. I sense that these gifts are the only Christmas she will know. It took me back to my childhood shared with a hundred other children...many of us with no parents...whose Christmas came from Sunday School classes who drew names. We could ask for three things. Sometimes we got all three...sometimes maybe one. I still have an old Bible with the print almost too small to read, the cover in bad repair, and my name misspelled on the front. But, it was a gift I asked for and received, and my heart was happy. I couldn't help but wonder as I wrapped for Stephanie how those Bible Class "angels" must have felt wrapping for us so long ago.

## A Child, the Wonder of Christmas and Cherished Memories

I thought also about a small green giraffe that I had been given at a Christmas party hosted by students at Wesleyan

Conservatory and how I cherished the giraffe and the love behind the gift.

## Friends Together

I received a note in the mail not long ago from a girl I'd grown up with and not seen for more than 40 years. She remembered. And, I received an invitation from the Children's Home to have a brick engraved with my name and placed among others in the Friendship Walk at the Home where we often gathered for watermelon cuttings, tacky parties on the 4$^{th}$ of July, summer night games, and so on. I asked for an engraved brick for my friend, Jossie, too, and asked that it be put close to mine since we were best friends then…and never far apart.

## Two Dollars and More

I think back to Christmas childhood as an "orphan kid" when one of the local dime stores would invite all of us from the Children's Home to come during Christmas and shop one early morning before school and before the stores opened for business. We'd go in with our $2.00 and somehow find a gift for each of our friends and have something left over for ourselves. Don't you find it's true that…when you share…you always have enough left over for yourself?

# *A Moment of Kairos*

### Edwin Chase

A blanket of leaves crunched underfoot as I walked toward fraternity row on the Emory University campus. After a sumptuous lunch of southern fried chicken with all the trimmings at the KA house, I prepared for an afternoon of study. After all, education was everything. That conviction was imbedded in my very marrow. Without education, one dug ditches. Simple and direct - cause and effect.

Heading toward the back door of the frat house to leave, I found myself summoned by Tommy Wilkens, a tall, lanky senior renowned for being an aristocratic intellectual who definitely marched to a different drummer, especially for 1962. Surreptitiously leading me into the hallway and looking over his shoulder as if to ensure that no one could hear us, Tommy unveiled the reason for his secrecy. "Buddy, I've never asked you to do anything as a pledge, so just do what I tell you," he whispered. "I want you to take the KA punch bowl and two dozen glasses to my house by eight o'clock this evening."

Stunned by his request, I attempted to explain that I had a biology exam the next morning. With "education first" as the motto of our fraternity, surely I would be released from this senior's demand. However, Tommy refused to budge and merely added, "The reception will begin at 8:30 tonight, and I want you there to serve. Wear a coat and tie. I know I can count on you." I could feel the anger in my throat, but I choked it back and nodded in agreement.

In our pantry, I located our exquisite sterling silver punch bowl and glasses and stashed them in the trunk of my car. Then I was off to the library to study.

That evening at the appointed time, I drove to Tommy's spacious house just off campus. Once the punch bowl was in place and the glasses arranged, I found a sofa in the living room and buried my head in my biology notebook determined to learn something for the exam in spite of my resentment at having to serve. I did not have long to study.

Startling me with his sudden appearance, Tommy commanded, "Start pouring the punch into the bowl. Folks will be arriving in a few minutes." There was obvious excitement in his voice.

"Who is going to be here tonight?" I ventured to ask.

"I've invited some professors and a black preacher from downtown," he barked as if I had exceeded some boundary of appropriateness. As he disappeared into the kitchen, I knew it was probably not a good idea to ask any more questions.

Soon a parade of prestigious professors from Emory began to arrive. Led by Dr. William Hocking, Dean of the School of Philosophy, the guests filled Tommy's spacious living room.

Presently, "the black preacher from downtown" entered the house.

Perfectly at home with professors and steeped in the theology of Paul Tillich and Reinhold Neibuhr, this preacher reminded me of the boy Jesus confounding the scribes in the temple. I was mesmerized by this man who possessed a passion for social justice and deep convictions about the sovereignty of God.

Our guest was calling for a radical paradigm shift, a new way of looking at the world. I wondered why as a child in Macon, Georgia, I had never thought it strange to see blacks seated in the back of a bus. Rather than entering into the discussion and revealing my lack of knowledge and experience, I was content to listen. I listened to the inescapable authority of this preacher whose words were wrapped in a melancholy that touched those who heard him.

Late in the evening a discussion ensued around the two Greek words for time: *chronos* for chronological time and *kairos* for God's time. He said emphatically, "When God breaks into human history, the *kairotic* moment is not often recognized until later." Little did I know he could have been talking about his message and himself.

As the guests were leaving, I shook the preacher's hand very much wanting to express my gratitude. But I simply said, "Good night, Dr. King."

Driving home, I considered the ironies of the evening. The sterling silver engraved KA punch bowl, a symbol of the Old Confederacy, had been used to honor a person who came to symbolize the Civil Rights Movement. Professors adorned in all the trappings of academia had been taught by one whose authority had not been recognized. Angry at having to put my books aside to serve punch, I had been gifted with an unforgettable experience in which my provincial ways of thinking had been exposed and challenged.

Six years later, when I heard that Dr. Martin Luther King, Jr., had been shot to death in Memphis, I wept. As the shock wore off, I was overwhelmed with the feeling that a bright light had been extinguished. For me, it continues to be a lifetime endeavor to remain true to the light of that memorable evening when our paths crossed.

# Chapter Eight

## *Rock and Roll on the Back Porch and Monopoly on the Front*

In the early 1950s country music wafted across the campus of the Home as children and staff enjoyed the music of Hank Williams and Roy Acuff. But it was Patsy Cline who sang her way into our hearts. In a few years this was quickly replaced by rock and roll with Elvis Presley and Buddy Holly who transformed the way American youth danced. In these years Lanier High School won state championships in football and basketball. Eisenhower was President. The country and the Home prospered.

In the late 50s just as folk music began to capture the attention of the country, our cows began to capture the attention of our neighbors as they watched their shrubbery being eaten. With pressure from the community, the Home shut down its dairy.

In the early 1960s the future looked promising as a youthful President Kennedy took office. There was even a fresh new sound in the air –The Beatles. The Home had seven students in college supported in part by the sale of pasture land that funded an endowment for education.

Then our secure world began to crumble. The Cuban Missile Crisis, the assassination of President Kennedy, the war in Viet Nam, racial unrest and violence, and the assassinations of Martin Luther King, Jr. and Bobby Kennedy caused many to despair. The challenge was to make sense of it all. Even in the worst of times, the Home was doing the best of things—caring for children, offering them a faith unshakable in adversity.

Circa 1951

**Welcome to the 1950s!**

In the 1970s board games like Monopoly began to give way to electronic games.  By 1976, the War in Viet Nam was over, Watergate had forced the resignation of a president and Jimmy Carter was in the White House.  Before his term was over, Islamic radicals had taken 52 American hostages that led to an oil embargo and gas shortages – a foretaste of things to come.  Meanwhile, the Home remained faithful to its mission – offering passionate and compassionate care to children and youth.

The stories in this chapter were lived out against the relatively calm years of the 1950s and the escalating turbulence of the following two decades.  In these stories the emotional impact of difficult decisions and surprise blessings are allowed to rise to the surface and find expression.

# *My First Sunday at the Home*

## Will (Willie) Blocker

During the summer of 1947, I entered the Methodist Children's Home in Macon, Georgia. I was a nine-year-old boy from the small South Georgia town of Faceville.

On my first Sunday Mrs. Clark, the junior boys' cottage matron, properly dressed me in borrowed clothes, and off we went to the Vineville Methodist Church, Macon's finest. Upon entering the sanctuary, I was struck by the bigness and beauty of it all. I had never before witnessed such splendor. The preacher and his assistant were dressed in pinstripe tuxedos with tails. All the choir members wore great flowing robes. There must have been a hundred of them standing up there on the beautiful maroon carpet.

Mrs. Clark sat beside me and kept a keen eye out for any misbehavior. I sat upright glancing about to take in all these new surroundings.

The preacher announced that Mrs. "Smith" would sing a solo. My only musical experiences up to now were gospel songs such as *I'll Fly Away*, *Amazing Grace*, and *Shall We Gather at the River* accompanied by the piano and guitar with lots of "Amens." On Saturday nights, I sat before a big upright radio and listened to the "Grand Ol' Opry" and "The Louisiana Hayride."

Mrs. "Smith" walked to the podium and began her solo presentation. To my young and unrefined ears, this lady seemed to be straining with each note. I'd never heard anything like it! Finally, when she hit a high quivering operatic note, I could contain myself no longer. A loud burst of laughter came from deep within. I thought, "This is about the funniest sound I've ever heard." With a quick elbow to the ribs, Mrs. Clark restored order, and the folks around us settled back into their pews. This was the first of many new experiences that would shape my life for years to come.

# A Little Boy Named Richard

## Carolyn Dozier Barfield

Sometimes extraordinary things can happen in ordinary places. There we would be, behind the kitchen peeling peaches. It doesn't get more ordinary than that. Then an old Cadillac would appear, and a young man named Richard Penniman would hang out as he waited for his aunt, Josie Cherry, our beloved cook, to walk through the door. He was there to drive her home.

Every now and then, as he waited, he would pull out his guitar and sing songs for us – Elvis Presley and Buddy Holly tunes. Attending these private concerts with me were Paulette and Betty Hughes and my sister Lena.

Years later, we were surprised to hear his voice again as Little Richard, the Rock and Roll star of the 50s and 60s.

So, I guess it pays to be in the right place regardless of how ordinary.

# *Fight'n Mad at a Funeral*

### Edwin Chase

I just knew him as "Mr. Ayers." He was the maintenance man at the Methodist Home. I got to know him because he drove the yellow school bus to Joseph Clisby School. But more than that, he was a friend to the children. His kind face and warm smile always said that this grandfatherly man was always available to hear what we had to say. On what seemed to me one of the worst days of my young life, Mr. Ayers was there to help me through it.

When I was in the second grade, the first time at Joseph Clisby School, I was not prepared for that lofty level of academic challenge. Adding three numbers was absolutely beyond me. When I brought home a report card indicating poor in every subject, Mrs. Ellis, the senior boys' matron, was determined that "her boys" could do better than that! But with me she had her work cut out. Once when I was trying to memorize the months of the year, I began just fine, "January…February… March…April…May…" After a pause, trying to help me, Mrs. Ellis asked, "Buddy, what is that bug that flies around here in June?"

I answered excitedly, "Oh yeah, a July fly!" Charlie Hall laughed so hard he fell out of his chair and had to stand in the corner.

In order to prepare me for my next spelling test, I was taught to memorize the letters in sequence for all the words on my next exam. Remarkably, after one week, I was ready. I knew all the words! I was excited and could not wait to pass my first test in the second grade!

Just before the test, as I was arranging my paper, I evidently brushed against the hair of the girl sitting in front of me. Indignantly, she spun around and shouted, "Stop it, Buddy!" I was immediately sent to the principal's office. Seeing the principal,

Ms. Allen, was not a big deal. I had been to her office often. She and I were almost on a first name basis.

There were tears in my eyes as I left the classroom, not because I had to go to the principal's office, but because I would not be able to take the test. By the time I was in the hallway, I was sobbing. As I turned the corner, there stood Mr. Ayers. Through a torrent of tears and words, I threw myself into his arms pouring forth my story. "I know all the words, and I can't take the test! It's not fair! I know all the words!" I blurted between gasps. My one chance to pass a test, and I end up in the principal's office! I had lost my opportunity to show the world, and especially myself, that I had at least learned how to spell. Mr. Ayers listened patiently and gave me a hug. That was all I really needed.

Not many months after my expulsion from class, Mr. Ayers died of a heart attack. I was devastated. He had been my friend; and for many of us, he had been like a grandfather. It was the first time anyone I knew personally had died. On the way to his funeral, I had a heavy heart and a lump in my throat. When the preacher stood up to speak, he quickly went from bad to worse. He looked funny, his hair was combed in a strange manner, and he used the word "ain't" twice. But, worst of all, he said the reason Mr. Ayers died was because he was a sinner. Now who was I to judge anything because, let's face it, that year I could not read, write, add, or subtract. But, I did know Mr. Ayers was a good man. If people died because they were sinners, there would be a lot more dead people in the world. Besides, I knew some old reprobates! It just didn't make sense. What that preacher said made Charlie Hall and me fighting mad!

Charlie leaned over and whispered in my ear, "I'm gonna whip his butt when this thing's over." I said I'd help. As the preacher continued to say that Mr. Ayers was a sinner, we got madder and madder. Charlie was looking at him with his eyes squinted, pounding his fist into the palm of his hand, saying over and over, "I can't wait to get him." Charlie, who later became an outstanding athlete, was a tough kid even as a fourth grader.

After the funeral service, we looked everywhere for the preacher. We searched and looked outside only to see a row of shiny black cars. By this time, Charlie was like a roaring lion, looking for a preacher to devour. But we couldn't find that funny looking man. Because it was our first funeral, we didn't know that the "fraidy-cat" preacher was in one of the black limousines. We finally gave up our attempt to find the weasel, which, in our eyes, made that preacher the luckiest man in Macon, Georgia.

As we were driving back from the funeral, I discovered that I felt much better than I had before the service. There was no sense of heaviness, and the lump in my throat was gone. In a strange way, getting mad at the preacher seemed to help me.

Fifty years later as I reflect on this experience, the preacher actually did us a favor by getting us all worked up. In expressing our anger and outrage, we were actually entering into the grieving process. I tell clients every week, "Feelings that aren't expressed become depressed." And, anger is an important aspect of the grieving experience. Getting fighting mad, in a curious way, fulfilled for me the promise of the fourth beatitude: "Blessed are those that mourn, for they shall be *comforted.*" God sometimes works in mysterious ways.

## *Grafting More than Camellias*

### Grover C. Lovett

When I arrived at the Methodist Home, I was in trouble most of the time.  Mr. Durden, the Superintendent, didn't know what to do with me.  When I was a teenager, one day he took me to the park, a lovely place on our campus, planted in azaleas, gardenias and camellias, and taught me how to graft camellias.

We would take a small piece of new growth from a white camellia, make an incision into a solid red camellia bush and implant the small shoot.  We bound it in place so the nutrients of the red plant would nourish the small shoot from the white one.  The result would be a big red blossom with a splash of white…a thing of exquisite beauty…a wonder of God's creation.

On more than one occasion, our camellias won first place in competitions all across Georgia.

**The Methodist Home grew much more than camellias.**

In many ways, my life is like one of those grafted camellias. In my early years at the Home, I was wild and rebellious.  Over time some positive character traits, a good work ethic, and some spiritual values were grafted into me. And, like a graft, I thrived in my new setting. Later, those character traits and values blossomed into a new life – leading me to a wonderful wife, great friends, and a rewarding career. These, too, were wonders of God's creation.

I'm grateful to the Methodist Home for seeing the good in me and bringing out the best. And, from what I understand, there is still a lot of grafting going on at the Methodist Home as children and youth continue to flourish and thrive in that sacred soil of love, encouragement, and spiritual vitality...a wonder of God's creation.

# *Fisticuffs*

### Edwin Chase

Fighting is simply a form of communication—an aggressive one, but communication nevertheless. As just about any youngster intuitively knows, fighting can be a method to make a point, to get across an important message, which if expressed in any other way, would seem lost to both sender and receiver. Fighting comes in all shapes and forms, ranging from the serious to the comical.

During one of those crisp fall afternoons when adolescent boys daydream of engaging in more manly and exciting endeavors than completing their assigned chores, my brother Billy and I, as well as several other boys at the Home, were raking leaves beside the little girls' cottage. Tim, who was a little younger than Billy and I, stunned us with his audacity by lighting up a cigarette. More than anything else, we all knew the gesture was an act of pure defiance against the rules strictly prohibiting such behavior. As if that were not a sufficient demonstration of his rebelliousness, Tim, who was standing near my brother, blew smoke directly into his face.

Billy's response was immediate. "Don't blow smoke in my face!" he commanded while glaring at Tim, who seemed to pay him no attention at all. In fact, Tim inhaled again, and this time no one could ever doubt that he intentionally blew smoke in Billy's face.

"You do that again, and I'll knock your block off!" Billy roared right in Tim's face. Sensing trouble brewing, the other boys and I stopped raking. Undaunted, Tim blew smoke again but this time into my brother's ear.

Handing me his rake, Billy stood in front of Tim, his arms folded. And, quick as a flash, Billy's right fist slammed against Tim's chin sending boy and cigarette backwards to the ground.

Trying to regain his composure and scrambling to his feet, Tim loudly pronounced, "You missed."

The look on Billy's face was one of incredulity. I could not believe my ears. Shrugging his shoulders, Billy turned as if to walk away. Then with a full back swing, Billy unloaded a right cross sending Tim once again to the ground. This time he did not get up. Lying face down, Tim muttered under his breath just loud enough for all of us to hear, "You missed."

Billy raised his eyebrows high as if to say, "He's crazy!" Then he burst out laughing. We all joined in and laughed so hard we would've fallen on the ground had we not been leaning on our rakes. There were no more punches thrown that day.

That autumn afternoon Tim provided us with a perfect example of bold-faced denial. He used denial as a way of coping with a reality that was unacceptable to him. Through the years, as I have thought about that incident with Tim; I have been confronted with my own need to deny, saying to a loss, a heartache, or a disappointment, "You missed. You can't touch me." All of us boys raking leaves that day were from broken homes and were separated from our parents. Underneath our tough exteriors was a reservoir of pain and sadness. Denial was our way of keeping that pain at a distance.

Even as an adult, I catch myself every now and then talking a lot of bravado as if I had not been knocked off my feet by some circumstance or feeling. And, I suppose, one measure of maturity is the ability to feel and express pain. This takes an enormous effort, especially for men. It's much easier to say, "You missed."

# The Lunch That Carried Me to North Carolina

### Edwin Chase

As I walked down Cherry Street in Macon, I had a decision to make: I could drop in at NuWay for lunch or catch a bus, ride home and eat in our dining room at the Home. I caught a bus and arrived just in time for a great lunch. But it would be no ordinary meal.

I noticed we had some visitors that day. As I was leaving, I was introduced to Mrs. Lillian Seville from Athens. After chatting with her for a few moments, she took me totally by surprise by asking, "Buddy, how would you like to work for me this summer at Lambuth Inn at Lake Junaluska in North Carolina?"

Wide eyed, I asked, "The whole summer?"

She answered, "Yes, you would live at the hotel, have your meals there, and I'll pay you $1,500."

I responded, "Sounds great!" Actually, it exceeded great. I spent the best two summers of my high school years working as a bus boy at Lambuth Inn. But work was only a small part of what was on the menu. Inspiration was the appetizer. New friends, the dessert. But fun was always the main course.

One evening in late June I helped a bell hop at Lambuth unpack his radio transmitter. We attached the antenna to the radiator system of the hotel. From a small room on the first floor, I stood before a microphone playing my guitar and singing songs on the air that could be picked up on radios as far away as Waynesville, North Carolina. We tuned the lobby radio to "our" frequency and entertained the guests. Walking by the radio, Mrs. Seville once quipped, "That sounds just like Buddy." Had she known the truth of her statement, I would have been fired on the spot.

We even wrote our own commercials advertising fictitious brand names: "I've been using Sunny Smile toothpaste all my life.

And all I've got to say is, 'Gimme back my teeth!'" When we gave out our call letters on the air (WLAMBUTH), the lifeguards at the Terrace Hotel picked up our signal, raced over, and joined the fun.

While working at Lambuth, I served Billy Graham, George Beverly Shea, and enough bishops to play several games of chess. I grew to love North Carolina and later, as an adult, took my family there for vacation every summer for seventeen years. Thanks to the generosity of Mrs. Courtney Gaines of Savannah, my family enjoyed spending the week in her six-bedroom summer home overlooking the lake. On her spacious front porch, we relaxed, sang songs, ate lunches and dinners, chatted with friends, and planned new adventures. We hiked the trails of the Blue Ridge Mountains, swam in cold, clear mountain pools, and fished the streams. The cool summer nights, silver queen corn, and trips to Granny's Chicken Palace, kept us coming back. When I see Lambuth Inn today, I remember with appreciation those magical summers of 1958 and 1959. I am so glad I went home for lunch!

# *Friendship at Georgia Boys' State, 1957*

## Bill Chase

In the summer of 1957, Charles Hall and I were among Lanier High School's group of rising seniors who attended Georgia Boys' State. The event was held at Georgia Tech in Atlanta. We considered it an honor to be selected to join 300 plus students from across Georgia to attend the week's learning experience about the state's political process. We toured state offices, talked with government officials and studied political processes. One of the activities was student elections for political offices, and the boys of Lanier plunged right in.

Hunt Sanders ran for Governor, Gene Bishop ran for Lt. Governor, Charles Hall ran for Treasurer, and I ran for Justice of the Supreme Court. "There are seven seats on the Supreme Court; seven chances to win a court nomination," I chuckled to Charles.

Because of the large number of schools and with only a handful of students from each school, there was no easy way to "become known" in a short time. Campaigning for office covered maybe two days and mainly consisted of placing campaign posters across campus and meeting as many people as possible.

Campaign posters had to be handmade, and we did not have a lot of time. The poster making became a chore for non-artistic me. But, I figured a few catchy posters could win the day if they brought name recognition. When things rhyme, they can be remembered, so I set about creating phrases that rhymed with my name, such as "Get on the pace, vote for Chase." I showed some of my posters to Charles.

"Oh, I get the idea," said Charles, "Don't mind the face; vote for Chase." Charles slapped his knee and laughed himself right out of his chair. Charles regrouped and was so amused with this idea that he begun drawing a cartoonist version of my face on a poster. He already had a number of well-made posters for his own

Treasurer's campaign; and, because he is an excellent artist, his posters drew attention fast. "Here's your big nose and down here is your jutting chin," Charles said, and we both laughed uncontrollably. Charles added the funny rhyme, and we both agreed that he had created a very amusing poster – probably the best one done all evening. I thanked Charles for his help, and I made sure this special poster went near the cafeteria entrance.

Circa 1957

**Charles Hall (center, back row) demonstrated to a pal what friendship was all about.**

In a few days, the elections were held. As chance would have it, I won the election, while my Lanier classmates did not. Charles lost his bid for Treasurer by two votes. I was one of the top vote-getters in the entire election; and, because I received more votes than the others who were elected as Supreme Court Justices, I was elected *Chief* Justice of the Supreme Court.

I believe I won the election because of Charles' funny-face poster, and I have always wondered if Charles could have picked up two or more votes and won his contest had he made just one more poster for himself instead taking time to help me. However, his sacrifice cemented a friendship that has lasted a lifetime.

# *Grace in the Fourth Grade*

## Bill Chase

I looked at the report card again. I was shocked—all G's. I turned the card over in my hand to see whose name was on the front. It was my report card all right. I looked at the final six weeks column again. The letters were neatly and clearly written— "G's" (good) alongside every subject. The other columns also summed up the other five grading periods in Miss Gibson's 4<sup>th</sup> grade class at Joseph Clisby Elementary School in Macon, Georgia. My grades were mostly average with some poor marks. What had I done to deserve a perfect report card? The answer: Nothing.

With surprise written all over my face, I took the card to the parking lot. The school bus was waiting to take the boys and girls back to the Methodist Children's Home where we lived. We climbed on the bus with our usual shouting, shoving, and arm hitting. Spirits were high as this was the last day of school, and the anticipation of summer was at hand.

Patsy, sitting in the seat in front of me, turned and asked, "What did you make on your report card, Billy?" It was the question I had learned to hate because it gave opportunity for the good students to brag and for the weaker students to be humbled. I had learned at an early age how people could set you up by asking questions. This time was going to be different. I decided to brag. "I made all G's," I replied with a smugness that was unreal.

"You did not. You are lying, Billy! You did not make all G's!" Patsy shouted. I didn't expect her to announce my grades to a whole bus load of children. I was feeling flushed because I was not familiar with this kind of attention. I had been indifferent about school, but this perfect report card was beginning to make a difference in my outlook.

"So what?" someone growled a few seats back. I turned and looked at Willie, a sixth grader. His blue eyes were clear and not as threatening as his voice had been. He had more to say, "You're in Miss Gibson's class, aren't you?"

"Yes," I replied, wondering how he knew my teacher's name.

"On the last six weeks' report card, Miss Gibson gives *everybody* all G's," he said matter-of-factly.

I didn't want to believe him. Why was he being so cruel? I withdrew to my thoughts. Willie was probably right. His reason made sense. I had not studied much and didn't do anything special in class. I certainly didn't deserve a perfect report card.

Circa 1952

**Billy Chase Studying**

By the end of summer, I had resolved that neither Willie nor anyone else would take away that good feeling of receiving all G's. That special feeling of perfection was addictive and became a potent driving force within me. This force grew to be a powerful motivator that led me to work hard at developing good study habits. These traits resulted in high school graduation with honors, a college education, a rewarding career, and a terrific life.

I have often thought about this turning point in my life and Miss Gibson's special grace extended to an undeserving student. I never found out whether Miss Gibson had a tradition of giving perfect report cards to her students on the final six weeks' report. In a dream, I asked Miss Gibson why she rewarded me with perfect grades for sub-standard performance. She smiled and said, "I learned this from my Father. You received a taste of grace for your average performance in school. How much greater is my Father's grace when you accept His love and mercy."

# *Josie Cherry - A Saint in the Kitchen*

## C. L. Neville

The children who lived at the Methodist Home from the late 1940s to the early 1970s will tell you that Josie Cherry was always a source of encouragement. As a cook in the kitchen, Josie nourished "her children" with wonderful meals, but even more so she nourished their very souls. Her warm smile and bright eyes always showed how happy she was to see them. Even college students, when home for the weekend, would drop by just to visit with her.

Josie was noted for the special little things she would do for the children. Girls who worked in the kitchen tell stories of Josie secretly giving them treats to snack on back in their cottages. For one lad who could not eat bread pudding, Josie would bake, especially for him, a custard pie and have it placed in a similar dish so no one would ever know that C. L. was not eating his bread pudding. From time to time, children would bring Josie freshly-picked blackberries that she would transform into a delicious blackberry cobbler.

Josie Cherry was someone who always had time to listen to what the children had to say. She was genuinely interested in what was happening in their lives. As one kitchen boy said, "The best part of working in the kitchen was Josie Cherry." Even after children left the Home, they would make it a point to drop by the kitchen and visit with this very special person. After she retired, alumni would drive to her home off Ingleside Avenue to catch up on things or just talk about old times.

Josie Cherry loved the children at the Methodist Home, and they loved her. To them she was a hero, a saint and a legend.

Circa 1975

**Josie Cherry's love of children healed a thousand wounds.**

# *Growing Up Strong and Straight*

## Nelle Ezelle Ayers

I have fond memories of the Methodist Home. I thank the Lord every day and count my blessings for all the wonderful things that the Home did for me. I am grateful for having the opportunity to have grown up in a home environment, and I am proud of what I learned. I would not have met my wonderful husband nor have my three beautiful children if it had not been for Mr. Woodall and the staff who taught me right from wrong, how to be polite and courteous to others, and to always be kind to others.

At the Home, we had certain chores to do. For instance, we were taught to cook and clean. I remember having to get up at 6:30 A.M. when it was my turn to cook breakfast and go to the kitchen to prepare eggs and help the cook with other breakfast items. When we were not scheduled to cook, we would go to the tennis courts and play tennis, or volleyball, or play a game of horse with the basketball.

We attended Vineville Methodist Church and were allowed to participate in a variety of activities. We were in church every Sunday morning and at the Methodist Youth Fellowship on Sunday nights. We were afforded the opportunity to have swimming lessons. Once we learned to swim, we were allowed to venture into the deep part of the pool. We always looked forward to Mr. Woodall calling us around 2:00 o'clock in the afternoon to go swimming. The time just before swimming was supposed to be our "quiet hour," but most of us already had our bathing suits on. When the call came, we were always ready.

I am so appreciative of having the opportunity to finish school and then go to Crandall Business College. It was rough getting up in the mornings and walking from the Home to the bus stop on Vineville Avenue to catch the city bus to go to Crandall, but it all paid off. After finishing Crandall, I was allowed to stay on campus until I could find a job.  I found one with the Macon Area Vocational-Technical School and began my new life outside the Home.

# A Fairy Tale with a Bump in the Road

## Nelle Ezelle Ayers

In late December 1953, the Superintendent of the Methodist Children's Home in Macon appeared at the door of the home of "Aunt Sis" in Toomsboro, Georgia. My two sisters and I had been living there due to the illness of our mother. We soon learned that this stranger had come to take us away to a new and unknown place where we would live without other relatives. Of course, we were terrified. We protested, ran, and hid ...to no avail.

After we arrived in Macon, the Superintendent, Mr. Woodall, took us downtown to Sears Roebuck and bought us some new outfits. The only clothes we had were the ones that we were wearing. From there we went to the Home and were taken to our designated cottages. My sister Mavis and I were placed in the same cottage. Mary Sue was assigned to the senior girls' cottage. We, of course, didn't like that. We feared that they were going to lock us up in rooms and keep us from ever seeing each other again. However, the doors weren't locked at all, and we often saw Mary Sue. Stranger still, although we arrived after Christmas, we were allowed to participate in Christmas by picking out several items that we liked, which were on display. The Home then gave us these presents to keep as our very own. We had never had Christmas at home.

Yet the sudden transition was hard for us. For about six months, Mavis hid behind doors and cried all the time. To comfort her, I would lie facing her at night, and we would hold hands until we fell asleep. We finally adjusted to our new environment. Soon we began to love it. We felt so fortunate to be living in such a nice place.

At the beginning of the third grade, I came down with a serious virus, which made my fingers peel and my feet swell. After staying in bed for several weeks, it was determined that I should be admitted to the Macon Hospital. I was hospitalized for a very long time. I was not allowed to sit up because my feet would swell. At first no one told me how serious my illness was. I lay in the hospital bed feverishly hearing choirs of angels singing. I had contracted rheumatic fever.

After several weeks, I was sent to the Elk's Aidmore Hospital in Atlanta. There I remained for the entire third grade. Mr. Woodall would make regular visits whenever possible and brought my sisters to see me. During my stay in Atlanta, I was able to keep up with some school assignments. One interesting thing I remember was a visit from the Cisco Kid and Poncho. This was a real treat for the children in the hospital.

When I was released from the hospital, I was able to return to school with certain limitations. I could not climb any steps or participate in strenuous activities. I entered Joseph Clisby School again and was assigned to a classroom located downstairs, which would be easily accessible to the lunch room and the outside for recess. I made regular visits to the doctor and was on medication for several years. I later regained my full strength and resumed normal activities. The care and concern of the Home I had once so feared had saved my life.

# Blue Bird on My Mind

### Edwin Chase

The excitement of graduation was over.  The gown had been returned.  Presents opened.  High school was officially behind me; college was before me.  And the only thing standing between me and college was the summer season.  But this was to be no ordinary summer.

During this time I had to earn as much money as possible.

Charles Hall, one of my friends at the Home, worked two summers at Blue Bird Body Company in Ft.  Valley, Georgia.  Yes, they are the folks who manufacture the ubiquitous yellow school buses.  I had visions of slaving away on an assembly line; but that was not to be.

I was assigned a job in upholstery.  However, I didn't work with fabric, foam cushion or padding.  I worked with the springs in the seat cushions.  But here is where things get interesting.  The springs arrived at Blue Bird in crates with 15 sets of springs stacked one upon the other.  Yet the crates were so compressed, they were a mere ten inches tall!

The springs were under tremendous pressure! My job was to liberate the springs from their cramped quarters and live to tell the story.

- I would place a crate of springs in a small machine especially designed to hold the crate secure.
- Then cut the wires that held the highly-compressed springs.
- Step behind a small protective wall.
- Then flip a switch.

When I flipped the switch - BANG! The pent up energy in the springs sent them sailing forty feet into the air in *all* directions.

When I was sure that all the springs had descended, I would come out of my hiding place, gather them up and stack them neatly in the corner.

I did this all summer. Eight hours a day. I had a lot of time to think about my future. By the end of the summer I knew one thing for certain: *I did not want to work in a factory!* I knew I'd better buckle down and study when I arrived at Emory and not squander this opportunity. I had always heard: "Education is everything." And after a summer of watching springs forever bouncing to heaven and falling to earth, I was eager to pursue my studies.

Courtesy of Erwin Harrison

**Who would have guessed that making a bus seat could be such an exciting venture!?!**

Blue Bird was a fine place to work. The bosses cared about their employees. Safety was always first. I vividly remember that once a week the assembly line would come to a screeching halt and time would be set aside for all employees to hear the encouraging words of a minister or a missionary.

In a business where the bottom line is *everything*, Blue Bird continues to march to a different drummer. And God has blessed this company that at the time was largest school bus manufacturer in the world.

The journey from childhood to adulthood is arduous. And those of us who worked at Blue Bird took some important steps in that journey as we learned a good work ethic that served us well, not only in college, but all the days of our lives.

# *Thanks for the Simple Things*

## Ann Rowland

The fondest memories of our lives are often the smallest, unspoken things.

My fondest memory is very simple, but comes straight from a loving heart.  It is of a plate of homemade oatmeal cookies and a glass of cold orange juice.

The wonderful hands that made these cookies for us were those of our sweet houseparent, Vinnie Newton.  I remember coming to the Methodist Home at the age of five.  At that time, I was very fearful.  However, through her love I began to feel right at home.  She always took the time to show each child a special kind of love.  Almost every day after school, we would return home to find that plate of homemade oatmeal cookies and a glass of orange juice.

Now that I'm grown and have children of my own, it really warms my heart to know that Vinnie Newton took a little extra time for all of us.  I know that all the extra things were done out of love.  From this fond memory comes thanks to Mrs. Newton for all the love she gave through such things as the cookies and juice.  And, to all the houseparents of the past and the present, I want to say children will *always* remember your love for them - even in the smallest things.  They never go unnoticed.

# *Ragamuffin Champs*

## Edwin Chase

We always thought of ourselves as decent athletes. We played every sport under the sun on the athletic fields of the Children's Home. We even played "rough-house tackle" daily without helmets, shoulder pads, or any other protective equipment. But, our athletic abilities had never been tested in the wider community.

Out of the blue, we received a challenge from another children's home in Macon to play a game of football on a Saturday afternoon at Baconsfield Park. Accepting the challenge was our first mistake. Showing up was our second.

After our opponents (who looked more like the Green Bay Packers) easily scored three quick touchdowns, I knew it was going to be a bad day. The comments made in our huddle are forever etched in my memory:

> "Knox, you run the ball!"
> "You're crazy. I just ran it."
> "Let's throw a pass."
> "Don't throw it to me!"
> "Me, neither!"
> "Okay. Someone get in the clear!" (No one did.)

When it was over, the score was 49 to 7. Charlie Hall scored our only touchdown on an intercepted pass. I remember the silence in the bus on the ride home. I was low and ached all over. But what really hurt was the sting of humiliation. I made a commitment to myself that I would never be so unprepared for a sporting event again. (I kept that commitment until the day I walked onto a golf course.)

Not long afterward, Mr. Rene Lanier, a prince of a man who was the Farm Superintendent and a role model and hero for an entire generation of young men, began taking us to the YMCA to play basketball on Friday evenings. Over time, we learned to love the game of basketball and began to excel as we honed our skills playing on the Lanier Junior High and Lanier Senior High teams. We focused on shooting, crisp passes, and aggressive rebounding. We also practiced on a makeshift goal behind what is now the Social Services Building.

Circa 1954

**Can anything good come from this group of ragamuffins?**

A few years later, the same children's home that had trounced us in football challenged us again – this time to play basketball with them in their new gymnasium. When we arrived, my heart sank. They had spectators; we had none. They wore uniforms; we looked like a team of ragamuffins in T-shirts and tennis shoes. It was beginning to feel like another humiliation might spring upon us. But this night would be different.

At half time our opponents were in shock, looking at one another in dismay as if to ask, "Who *are* these guys?" We had arrived with a fire in our bellies and a score to settle. We were shooting seventy percent from the floor and grabbing most of the rebounds. In the course of the game, my brother Billy and I made the discovery that we could sense what the other was thinking. I could pass the ball to him without as much as a glance. He always knew when it was coming and took advantage of many an open shot. Charlie Hall, one of our best athletes, was a vacuum cleaner on the backboards. When the final buzzer sounded, we had soundly beaten them on their home court. I think we were as surprised as they were.

But out of respect, we delayed our celebration until we were in the bus and the door was closed. Then pandemonium broke loose. We pounded the sides of the bus and made noise most of the way home. After things settled, Rene Lanier, with tears in his eyes, told us how proud he was of each one of us. Inside we all grew six feet tall in one evening. We were ragamuffin champs!

# Chapter Nine

# *The Patches Continue in Wondrous Patterns*

From 1980 to the present one of the major changes to impact family life in America has been the *increase in violence.* Violent crime, violence in film, school shootings, and terrorist bombings, culminating in the terrorist attacks of 9/11, have left an indelible imprint upon family life.

As our world has increasingly become more violent, research shows that the American family has become more unstable and abusive, especially in families where there is an absentee father. Against a background of increasing violence, Steve Rumford, who was installed as CEO at the Home in 1984, among other improvements, initiated a new ritual – the giving of a handmade quilt to every child who arrived at the Home.

Mr. Rumford challenged churches and anyone interested to make and send quilts, a challenge that received an immediate response. Exquisite quilts began pouring in from churches across South Georgia and later from around the country. In a world where children are often treated as expendable, the gift of a handmade quilt says, "You are someone special and unique, like the quilt you hold in your hand."

In the first chapter the question was raised, "Whose children are these?" And the answer was given in the little things, the care, the love, the encouraging word; and in a beautiful and symbolic way, the giving of a quilt to a child that says quietly: "These are *our children.*"    Like a sacrament, the quilt is a physical manifestation of the love and affection that surround the children who receive care at the Home.

Quilts are sacred.  In a family it is a quilt that is often passed down from generation to generation.  It is kept until it's worn to shreds.  Ask Matt Pippin, who grew up at the Home.  After decades, his quilt is still one of his prized possessions.

Since 1984, some new patterns have been woven into the quilt that is the Home.  There have been seven new cottages and a school erected on the Macon campus.  In addition, in five communities across South Georgia there are now seven new cottages and five support facilities serving more than 250 children every day.

And once a year over Labor Day weekend patches of the quilt – those adults who grew up at the Home, travel from distant cities and gather for Homecoming.  They greet each other and talk of old times.  The richness of their stories inspired the creation of this book.    The stories in this chapter, some shared at Homecoming, take place in the midst of great upheaval.  They are stories of courage, love and grace.

# *A Broken-down Bus*

## Steve L. Rumford

God's watchful hand has always been a part of the Methodist Home.  At times, He intervened in a general way for the institution, but most often His actions were more personal.  In 1983, my wife Rozelle and I often prayed, asking God if we should remain at the Methodist Home for Children and Youth in Versailles, Kentucky, where I was Association Director, or if I should seek an Administrator's job at another United Methodist child-care agency.

Meanwhile, we were busy with the activities of the Kentucky Home.  In the spring we took twenty-six youth, three adults, and our children (three boys) to Florida on a camping trip and a visit to Disney World.  The first South Georgia church I ever entered  was Valdosta First United Methodist Church, where we spent a night in the fellowship hall on the way.

We returned a week later and planned to spend the night in the gym of the Mulberry Street United Methodist Church in Macon.  Traffic was terrible as a long, hard rain began to overflow the streets.  We also realized that we had a mechanical problem and stopped at a gas station just outside Vienna (about 35 miles south of Macon) at 8:55 P.M.  The man on duty was anxious to close and simply said, "I can't help you; I won't help you; and I don't know who *can* help you."  With that "good" news, we proceeded north for about three miles before the bus jerked to a stop and refused to move one inch farther.

Broken-down in a steady rain, my first goal was to keep the kids calm and wait for help.  When no help came, I climbed (with much apprehension) a fence and approached a farm house with dogs barking.  I had informed our youth that we belonged to a connectional church, and that we would call the local Methodist preacher.  A wonderful Baptist couple answered the door.  They knew the Methodist minister.  He answered the phone, and within twenty minutes Rev.  Joel Dent was not only with us, but had the best mechanic in Vienna with him.  Although the mechanic got the engine started, he felt that we should wait until morning to be sure that the bus was sufficiently repaired.

Courtesy of Erwin Harrison

**For Dr. Steve Rumford a broken-down bus became
a date with destiny.**

The minister was great.  We got the girls and female staff into a motel, and Rozelle and I and all the boys slept at the church. Reverend Dent and I bought hamburgers for everyone; and since we were both Asbury graduates, we talked past midnight.  All went well the next morning, and by 9:00 A.M. we were on our way.

That following March I was at the Methodist Home in Macon interviewing for the Administrator's position.  I really questioned why and if this position was right for me.  I had many doubts and wished that I could somehow have a "sign." Leaving Kentucky was a major life decision, and we knew so little about Georgia. To us, Macon was the S&S dinner break on the way to Florida.

All that changed when I walked into the dining room to have lunch with the interview committee and saw the other applicants and one interviewer in particular: Joel Dent. I had my sign. Joel approached me and asked, "Don't I know you?" I was amazed.

I responded with, "Yes you do! You are my Guardian Angel." At that point, I was no longer there to interview, but to claim the job God had prepared.

I have always looked at that day as a defining point in my professional life. Twenty years later, I remember each of the individuals on that interview committee with great awe and tremendous respect. They have now become my long-time good friends.

# *Unconditional Gifts of Love*

## Tonie Maxwell

As Secretary to Steve Rumford, President of the Methodist Home, it is my privilege to handle the processing of the beautiful quilts donated for the children at the Home. Every quilt is so different. It's always exciting to see the design and handiwork of each one. With our note of thanks, I always include a copy of the poem, *Wounded Souls, Dried Tears and Quilts*, written by Gary Lister that was dedicated to the residents, staff and quilt-makers of the Methodist Children's Home in Macon. His poem has a way of pulling the threads of this ministry together.

The quilts are numbered as they come in with the oldest numbers being placed on quilt racks in Mr. Rumford's office for the children's selection. After a quilt is received and before it makes it to the quilt rack, it is displayed in the various offices on campus for everyone to see. There is even a quilt rack in the dining hall that keeps a seasonal quilt on display all year round.

Recently, one of our alumni, Matt Pippin, stopped by for a quick visit. As I was showing him a special quilt we had recently received, he remarked: "I have literally worn my quilt out; for years I took it everywhere I went."

I guess my favorite part of the quilt process is to "listen in" as Dr. Rumford allows a child to choose a quilt when he or she first comes to the campus. I always look forward to the way he presents the quilt to a child.

**Heidy receives her quilt as she and Dr. Rumford stand in front
of the 1,000th quilt donated to the Home.**

He tells them, "Every quilt is different and special just as you are. The quilt is your keepsake to cherish and take care of just as you are to cherish and take care of yourself. This is our way of saying we care."

---

### *Wounded Souls, Dried Tears and Quilts*

**Written by Gary Lister**

They arrive, tender young souls,
wounded almost beyond hope,
reaching desperately for any kindness,
like a shipwrecked man grasps
the tiniest flotsam, hoping against hope
to find something to bear his weight.

The Methodist Children's Home may be their last hope.
Painfully separated from everything familiar,
they arrive tentatively, expecting a continuum of pain.
They're met instead with love, someone has anticipated
their arrival long before, and created with kind,
gentle hands, a quilt for them alone.

Dry your tears, child. We're all family here.
You are loved and treasured, see, here's the proof.
Accept this quilt as evidence of things
not seen, wrap yourself in comfort and care.
When you need a reminder that you are not alone,
look, it's right there on your bed.

---

The Home is a wonderful organization that truly cares about the lives of children, and every quilt speaks eloquently of that care. I feel blessed to be a part of this outstanding organization.

# *Hearing the Story for the First Time*

## Rick Lanford

Two weeks before Christmas I overheard one of our volunteers who serves as receptionist say, "'Daddy Rick' is right here, would you like to speak with him?" Taking the phone and hearing the voice of concern on the other end of the line quickly removed any notion that this was a donor who wanted to make a contribution to the Home.

The principal of one of our elementary schools had called and asked me to please drive to the school and pick up Donald. "He's been fighting," she said factually, but upset. She was concerned, but I was stunned. "Wait, are you sure it is Donald who was fighting?" Several boys from the home could engage in a little roughhousing, but Donald was not among them – at least, not to my knowledge. Donald was a stout, subdued, and sedate young boy. "It was Donald," she responded, a sharper edge now to her tone. "You need to come get him."

The only thing more surprising than Donald fighting was the scene awaiting me in the principal's office. As I walked through the door, I observed Donald sitting alone at a table, his head buried in his arms. Six other teachers stood in a semicircle around him. Some of them appeared disheveled and exhausted. Their posture looked as though they feared Donald might erupt again. I could not imagine Donald creating such chaos.

Naturally, I was eager to hear the principal's account of Donald's behavior. As she shared the story, my surprise promptly turned to sadness. His teacher had made a rather benign request: Each student was to write a one-page essay about their Thanksgiving celebration with their family. No child in the class could have felt more uncomfortable than Donald. For a ten-year-old boy, new to the Methodist Home, such an assignment would have caused a churning of emotion deep within his soul. Donald's greatest fear was having attention drawn to the fact that he did not live with his family.

A classmate had teased Donald saying, "You don't have anything to write about because you don't have a family. You live at that orphanage." Theologian Jurgen Moltmann once wrote that our past can act as a thorn, creating an opening in the flesh, allowing the dynamics of the past to enter the present. Donald's classmate used Donald's past like a thorn, opening a wound in Donald's heart in the presence of his peers. His repressed feelings bled into that moment and Donald unleashed years of pain. It took six teachers to subdue Donald and stop the fighting.

I felt for the teachers forced to handle Donald that day. I also felt for Donald. He needed to learn respect for authority and how to manage his feelings. I offered Donald two options.

First, he could refuse to cooperate, and I would physically pick him up and place him in my truck; or secondly, he could act like a gentleman, apologize to the teachers for his disruptive behavior and use of colorful language and walk to the truck with me. Donald's head stayed fast upon his left arm while he lifted up his right arm and held up two fingers. You could almost hear a combined sigh of relief as he opted for the second possibility. Donald stood, and bravely apologized and walked quietly to the truck. On the trip back to the Home he was again the quiet, somber Donald.

He was suspended from school for three days. Children at the Home who are suspended are assigned productive tasks around the campus. Donald was to work for the maintenance department. He was to put out the nativity display for Advent and Christmas. As I turned into the entrance of the Home that morning, I was shocked to view one of the wise men from our nativity display standing in the flower bed. I slowed and eyed a second Magi on the porch of the Administrative Building. My shock reached its culmination when I observed Donald dragging an object up the hill, in the middle of the drive way into the Home. I pulled alongside him, lowered my window and asked, "Donald, what are you doing?" In frustration he answered, "I am putting these old men out!"

I could not help but stifle a chuckle. Not only was his choice of words comical, the way he held the last Magi was hilarious. In a hold that would make a professional wrestler proud, Donald held the last Magi around the head in a headlock. The humor of that moment quickly faded when it occurred to me that Donald needed to know whom he was carrying. I addressed him again, "Donald, do you know who these men are?" Donald spoke with a slight lisp and answered,

"No s. . .thur."

I told him about the Magi and the important role the wise men played in the story of Christ's birth. When I finished his countenance had softened; his words touched me. "'Daddy Rick,' no one has ever told me that story before." I no longer needed to worry about stifling my laughter; I was holding back tears.

Later that year Donald gave his heart to Jesus and was surprised to discover that even Donald was a beloved member of God's family! The next year when he played one of Magi in the Christmas pageant, he was pleased to give his special gift to the Christ child.

Every Christmas I have the privilege of reminding our staff of the Home's mission and why we give, not only our gifts, but ourselves to our ministry. We listen to our children, learning of their joys and their sorrows. Furthermore, we tell the story of Jesus without apology. It is our sacred commitment that no child in our care ever has to say, "No one has ever told me about that before."

# *Agents of the Home*

## Steve L. Rumford

Since its very beginning, the Methodist Home has always had an ordained Elder of the South Georgia Conference in the position of fund raiser/agent/liaison. In those early years the Home relied on goods, produce, and other donations from across South Georgia. In the fall railroad cars would be available for churches and families to bring canned goods, preserves, cotton, clothing, coal, gifts, homemade soap and syrup to be taken to Macon. It was in the 1890s when the Home urged Methodists to donate a day's wages of work to the Home.

In the pre-World War I era, the price of cotton was in boom, and the Home did well. As the Depression took its toll, the Home's annual budget fell from $36,000 per year to just over $10,000. Rev. J. A. Smith, Agent for the Home, bemoaned the plight of this orphanage as not only donations plummeted, but no endowment existed for its "bulwark of safety and well being." In the early thirties, he shared with the Board that the Home was in perilous financial condition.

What should have been a great disadvantage was that J. A. Smith did not drive. He relied on rail travel to take him to towns across the Conference where ministers and friends of the Home would welcome him and take him to the various churches. He was in a church 50 weeks a year. On more than one occasion, he would announce that he had obtained five railroad passes (given to the Home), and that he could go to any railroad town in South Georgia.

In recent years Dr. Laudis "Daddy Rick" Lanford, has covered South Georgia in a diesel pick-up truck, preaching Sunday worship services, Wednesday night suppers, funerals, weddings and revivals.

On one week night Rick and I had been to a meeting and had several appointments in the Savannah area. We were coming back at about 9:00 o'clock in the evening when we got to Metter, Georgia, and had not eaten. We stopped at a steak house and found it pretty much empty. Eating in a restaurant with "Daddy Rick" is an amazing experience as he is a stranger to no one, knows everyone, and will witness to the glory of God in a heartbeat. When Rick was ordained, he indeed did claim the authority of the Lord Jesus Christ.

As we were working our way through the salad bar, we were quietly joined by someone who looked as mean as they come. He had on a camouflage hat that was worn and oily. He had a three or four day-old beard, wore fatigues, and for a final statement had a .38 automatic pistol on his hip. "Daddy Rick" looked him straight in the eye and as an opening "ice breaker" asked, "Where do you go to church?"

The ice did not break. A glare came back Rick's way and the comment was, "I don't go to church."

Rick quickly saw his opening and burst out with his voice clearly heard, "Why not?"

To which the response was a glaring and clear, "I've got my ways."

At that time, I nudged in between the two and whispered to Rick, "Witness to the ones who aren't wearing the guns." Twenty minutes later, I watched Rick as he was talking to the group the man was with. They were a SWAT team awaiting a helicopter piloted by a friend of Rick's to go on a drug raid.

The man did not warm up to Rick that evening; but, I have often thought if he ever needed a minister for a crisis, a funeral, or a wedding he could call on Rick.

# *From Misgivings to Joy*

## LaShanda F. Shuman James

I will never forget that day. What happened was so unexpected. The day began to go down hill when my phone rang. It was a staff member at the Methodist Home who told me to come to the Administration Building because Mr. Rumford wanted to see me. I had just returned from college.

I felt uneasy about going to meet with Mr. Rumford – mostly because I had no idea why I was being summoned. When I arrived at the Administration Building, he was standing on the porch waiting for me.

He looked at me straight in the eye and stretching out his hand, placed it on my right shoulder and said, "LaShanda, I've been hearing that you've been wearing the staff out by driving you to work and to other places. I called you here today to tell you that this will not need to happen again."

As Mr. Rumford paused, my palms began to feel sweaty and my mouth was dry. I said, "I'm sorry! I didn't mean to be a burden."

Mr. Rumford interrupted me saying, "I tell you what – I have a better idea. See that car over there?"

"Yes sir."

'Well, it's yours. Here are the keys. Now you can drive yourself to work and all over town."

Seeing the car keys in my hand, I realized that I had been called to the Administration Building *not* to receive a reprimand, but a *wonderful gift*! My eyes filled with tears and I thanked and hugged Mr. Rumford until he began to wilt.

A morning that began with misgivings soon became a day of thanksgivings, one of the best days of my young life.

**For LaShanda – just being near this car brings a pleasant memory and a smile.**

# *The Giving of the Quilts*

## Sandra Lee Pike

Shortly after arriving at the Home, I got into a fight with one of the girls in my cottage. That fight landed me in a youth detention center. While I was in the detention center, every child at the Home was given a quilt that the ladies from several churches had made. When I returned from the detention center, Mr. Steve Rumford called the entire campus to the front of the chapel. I was called to the top of the steps, and there I was asked to pick out my quilt in front of the whole assembly. This really made me feel very special. To this day, I still have that quilt and the pillow to match it.

I don't regret being in the Home at all. I wouldn't change a thing because I have so many memories of those three wonderful years. Now, as an adult, I have grown to appreciate the staff members more. I want to say a big "Thank You" to all the kids and staff from the years 1984-1987. Without you, I wouldn't have the memories that I now cherish in my heart.

# Carried Safely Through the Flood of 1994

## Kim Hayes

When I took the job at the Methodist Home as Houseparent at the Americus Group Home in January of 1994, I had no idea how much that decision would change my life. Having just graduated from college, I was not really sure if this career was what I wanted to do with my life. But at the time, it seemed like a good opportunity.

On the night of July 5, 1994, I was just coming back to work after being away for a few days. Sherrell Bailey, a respite Houseparent, and I had some catching up to do. Mr. Rumford had visited us that afternoon and had taken us all out to eat. We assumed that it would stop raining later that day. It never did.

After we had gotten the girls to bed, I was about to turn in when Sherrell and I fell into a deep conversation. She filled me in on what had been going on in the cottage while I was away, including the news that we now had two new kittens. I knew Sherrell from church, but did not know her well. We swapped stories about our families and experiences. Our talk soon turned spiritual. She talked about heaven in ways that fascinated me. I had just started going back to church because that was one of my duties as Houseparent. We could hear the rain outside. It was an ominous, steady downpour.

Sherrell began telling me a story about shooting an intruder while she was babysitting. As if it were part of the script, the moment that she said this, lightening struck a tree outside, and the lights went out. The emergency lights in the hallway came on, but the living room remained very dark. I had a candle in my room and went to get it. By its light, we continued to sit and talk in the living room even though it was quite late.

During our conversation, I kept getting the feeling that I should go and check on the kittens. The feeling would not go away. The longer I sat on the couch, the more compelled I felt to go and check on those kittens. When I finally got up, I was shocked to discover that the carpet was wet. And worse yet, the water was coming into the house through the windows in the foyer! We called Judy Tott, the Director, and told her what was going on. She told us to get the girls up and get them to her house. Sherrell and I went to wake up the girls. We tried to explain to them as calmly as possible that we needed to get out of the house and go to Judy's.

By the time they were up and were getting dressed in the dark, the carpet in the back of the house was soaked and was beginning to puddle. Then Sherrell reported that she could not get any doors to open to the outside. I had to see for myself. I went to the fire door at the back of the house and tried to push it open. It would not budge. We did not know at this point that the house was already immersed in three feet of water. We were not getting out through a door. I went into the living room and pulled up the blinds. What I saw was indescribable. It was like an exhibit at an aquarium. I could see the top surface of the water and also underneath the water through the windows! Sherrell telephoned Judy again. She promptly called the police. Their advice was to climb up into the attic. This thought made me very uncomfortable. Judy called back and said that Dan Torbert, our electrician across the street, was going to come and help us. The girls were afraid, but not panicked. They were trying to stay calm, and all of us were trying to figure out what we were going to do. The lights were out, the water was now ankle deep, and we couldn't open any doors.

Soon we saw headlights in the driveway. By that light I discovered just how bad the storm really was. Our front yard was gone; in its place was a raging river. The phone rang, and Judy said that Dan could not see us in the house. The girls brought my candle to the window in the den. The unthinkable then happened. He left! When we saw his truck back out, we all started screaming even though no one could hear us. Judy told us that he was going to get help, but that didn't calm our fears. When he returned, he was alone.

Dan waded through the water to the windows in the kitchen. He told us that he would take one girl at a time through the chest-high torrent. We had one girl that could not swim and who was terrified of the water. We decided that she should go first in case we got stuck in the house. We put her up and through the window, and she slid into Dan's arms. Together they waded through the churning water to the other side. Each time I put a girl through that window I had to encourage and convince her that everything would be fine and that she would make it. And each time I held my breath until I saw them safely over. Dan was getting tired and moving slower to the other side. Water was over the heads of two or three of the little girls; they were dead weight as he carried them away from the house. He went under a couple of times, and it was obvious that our predicament was becoming more perilous. The water in the house was getting deeper, and the current outside was getting stronger. I felt that time was running out.

We placed the kittens in a Tupperware container; and as the last resident slid through the window, it sounded like the house was tearing apart. I pushed the resident out into the water and held onto the back of her shirt. Sherrell and I jumped into the kitchen sinks and then through the window into the water. Thankfully Dan was there and already had the resident in his arms. I don't remember how long it took to walk from the house to the higher ground. I do remember finally feeling safe and looking into the faces of my girls and rejoicing that we all had made it. That's all that mattered.

I found out later that the flood was caused by 23 inches of continuous rainfall across Georgia. Twenty miles to the east the Flint River had reached flood stage. However, in Americus our flooding was not caused by the Flint. It was caused by the overflow of 48 dams which sent water surging like some new river right through the Americus Group Home. Seventeen persons died in Americus and Sumter County in the early hours of that pre-dawn flood. Had it not been for Dan Torbert, who knows what might have happened to us.

The flood changed my life. Looking back over all the things that worked together to get us out of that house safely, I was astounded at God's providence. The emergency lights that were only supposed to burn for forty-five minutes provided light for two and a half hours. The one candle that I had saved burned for three hours. Having the electricity go out at the time it did was a blessing. I can't imagine what would have happened had the waters risen to the level of our electrical outlets. And although the power was out, the phone still worked. Finding Dan at home and his willingness to risk his life for ours was a Godsend. I shudder to think what might have happened had Sherrell and I gone to bed earlier that evening. What if I had not gotten up to check on those kittens? Had I been able to open a door, I doubt that we would have all made it out alive.

Circa 1994

**The young women rescued from the flood will never forget Dan Torbert's heroic actions.**

God was with us. That house was surrounded by God's angels, and there was no way that God was going to let anything happen to us. Through this experience, I rededicated my life to Him. God has given me a new appreciation for the gift of life...just how precious it is. But, that's not the end of the story. The generosity, love and kindness shown by the surrounding churches through their efforts to help us, clothe us, feed us, and find us a new place to live filled me with God's love all over again. I wasn't the only one touched by it. The girls saw a difference in their own lives. We will forever be bonded by the night of the flood...heroic Dan, courageous girls, and a night of God's grace and mercy.

# *About the Authors*

About the Authors

Please note that the dates in parentheses indicate the author's years in residency at the Home.

**Nelle Ezelle Ayers** (1953-1967)

Nelle lives in Warner Robins, Georgia, with her husband, James. In 2008 they celebrated their 40$^{th}$ wedding anniversary. For 32 years she worked in the field of Human Services with developmentally challenged children and adults. Now retired, she has ample time to enjoy her three sons and her seven grandchildren.

**Carolyn Dozier Barfield** (1953-1965)

Carolyn lives in Macon, Georgia, and has worked at YKK, USA, Inc. for 25 years. She is married with three sons, five grandchildren and one great-grandchild.

**Will Blocker** (1947-1951)

Will currently lives in Mooresville, N.C., with Loretta, his wife of 49 years. He worked for 24 years as a special agent with the Bureau of Alcohol, Tobacco & Firearms in Florida, Georgia, Alabama and North Carolina. They have four children and four grandchildren. Their oldest son, Phil, followed him into law enforcement and is a Captain at the Mooresville Police Department.

### Georgia Kent Boggs (1929-1937)

Georgia married and raised a large family. She taught Sunday School for 23 years. She was widowed in 1984 and currently lives in Steele, Alabama, enjoying her 15 grandchildren and 13 great-grandchildren.

### Bill Chase (1949-1962)

Bill lives in Macon, Georgia, with his wife, Joann. He served eight years as an officer in the United States Navy and worked for 33 years in Research and Development at Eastman Chemical Company in Kingsport, Tennessee. As a retiree, he is active in church and community. He is Secretary of the Methodist Home Alumni Association. Bill and Joann's son, Mark, works as a computer professional in Charlotte, North Carolina.

### Edwin Chase (1949-1965)

Edwin is a pastoral counselor who serves as senior chaplain and director of the Family Institute at the Methodist Children's Home in Macon, Georgia. Prior to coming to the Home, he served as director of the Clergy Resource Center, which he founded at the Pastoral Institute in Columbus, Georgia. Prior to that, he served for 14 years as a parish minister in Americus and Savannah. He is married to Carole Hoelle and has three sons and three grandchildren.

### Zimmie Irwin Goings (1942-1956)

After growing up at the Home, Zimmie graduated from Young Harris College, in North Georgia. She relocated to Washington, D.C., where she worked mostly in legal capacities until her recent retirement. Zimmie, her two sons and three grandchildren live in northern Virginia. She has been actively involved for years in her church's youth and worship activities, in costuming, and handbell ringing. She has authored five books.

**Charles Gordon** (1951-1962)

Charlie Gordon lives in Macon, GA, as do his two grown children, Chuck and Laurie. He has a grandson and a granddaughter. He has worked in the automobile business most of his life. Charlie coached baseball in the Vine-Ingle Little League, and son Chuck has also coached in this league for 18 years. Charlie now enjoys watching others play and coach at all levels.

**Kim Hayes** (Child Care Counselor)

Kim left the Methodist Home after 12 years of service when she and her husband, Kenny, moved to Florence, Kentucky. She is a service coordinator for Northkey Community Care.

**Bill Hill** (1926-1936)

Bill served in the United States Army in field artillery for more than twenty years and retired as a Master Sergeant. He served in Hawaii, Australia, Good Enough Island, New Guinea and the Philippines. After retirement, he worked for the MD&S Railroad. Bill is President of the Georgia Chapter 3, Pearl Harbor Survivors Association and is Vice President of the state chapter.

**Wallace L. Hubbard** (1929-1941)

After graduation from high school, Wallace served three years in the Navy. Following his time in the service, he married and began a career in the field of steam engineering working as a power house engineer for the General Motors Corporation. After 30 years, he retired in 1983 and currently lives in Hobe Sound, Florida.

## LaShanda F. Shuman James (1992-2001)

LaShanda is an Administrative Assistant in the Human Relations Department at the Methodist Home in Macon, Georgia. Prior to coming to the Home, she worked as a social worker for the Department of Family and Children Services at the Medical Center of Central Georgia. LaShanda is married and enjoys fishing with her husband.

## Catherine Johnson (1929-1939)

After her marriage to Van Johnson, she moved to Perry, Georgia, to assist her husband with the operation of a family-owned clothing store in downtown Perry. In 2006 she and her husband moved to a senior retirement center in Columbia, South Carolina. They celebrated their 67$^{th}$ wedding anniversary recently. She has two daughters and two granddaughters.

## Van Johnson (Husband of Catherine Wood Johnson, 1929-1939)

Van owned and managed Johnson's Store in Perry, Georgia, from 1940 to 1983. In 2006 he and his wife, Catherine, moved to a senior retirement center in Columbia, South Carolina. He has two daughters and two granddaughters.

## James Kent (1929-1940)

James retired from the U.S. Army as a Major after serving for 20 years. He then served as the CEO of the Talladega Chamber of Commerce for seven years. He taught at Gadsden State Junior College and served as President of the Alabama School for the Deaf and the Talladega Teachers Association. He married Helen G. Stines and has two daughters. He is currently retired and lives in Talladega, Alabama.

**Wiley J. Kent** (1929-1940)

Wiley joined the Army while at the Home. After basic training he was sent to North Africa where he was wounded in action. After his discharge, he began a lifelong career in the ceramic tile business, and for years owned his own company. At the time of his death, he had three daughters and five grandchildren.

**Rick Lanford** (Daddy Rick – President of the Methodist Home Foundation)

Rick is an ordained United Methodist minister and is the President of the Foundation of the Methodist Home. Prior to that he was Vice President of Development and Public Relations. Rick has served the Methodist Home for 14 years. He is married and has two daughters.

**Rene Lanier** (Farm Superintendent, 1948-1958)

Rene lives in Dalton, Georgia, with his wife, Maxine. After ten years as the farm supervisor at the Home, Rene Lanier became Superintendent of Cherokee Boys Estate in Dalton. As a retiree, he enjoys working in his gardens and spending time with his seven grandchildren and his three great-grandchildren.

**Grover C. Lovett** (1941-1953)

Grover lives in Savannah, Georgia, with his wife, Fae. He has been in the catering business for more than 45 years. He has two children, three grandchildren and five great-grandchildren.

**Tonie Maxwell (**Executive Secretary to Dr. Steve Rumford)

Tonie has worked as the Executive Administrative Assistant to the President of the Home since 1994. She and her husband Mike have been married for 35 years and have one daughter and two grandchildren.

**Walter Scott McCleskey** (A United Methodist Minister)

Walter Scott is a United Methodist minister who served as a Chaplain in the Army and later served a number of churches in the South Georgia Conference.

**C. L. Neville** (1953-1965)

C. L. lives in Macon, Georgia, with Lynn, his wife of 34 years. He is retired from the Georgia Air National Guard where he worked for over 35 years. As a retiree, he is involved in his church as well as volunteering his time for several charitable organizations. He is the President of the Methodist Home Alumni Association as well as an active board member on several local charity boards. He has two children.

**Sandra Lee Pike** (1984-1987)

Sandra returned to school and earned her G.E.D. and later received her CNA certificate. She is married and lives in Macon, Georgia.

**Mary Alice Hughes Roth** (1949-1964)

Mary Alice taught in Hapeville, Georgia, with the Fulton County School System for 33 years. She was named "Teacher of the Year" four times and was later named to "Who's Who Among America's Teachers." She and her late husband, Jack, have made Fayetteville, Georgia, home. She is active as a master gardener, church and community volunteer, and a member of a local ladies club.

**Ann Rowland** (1970-1980)

Ann Rowland lives in Hazlehurst, Georgia, with her husband and two daughters. After working as a pre-school director for many years, she now works with her husband in a family-owned insurance agency.

**Steve L. Rumford** (President/CEO, the Methodist Children's Home)

Steve has served as President and CEO of the Home since 1984. He has been involved in child care for over 40 years. He and his wife, Rozelle, have been married for 39 years and have four children and two grandchildren.

**Ida Ruth Sheffield Sanders**

The editors would be grateful to find how to contact the Sanders family. Ida is the daughter of one of the early residents of the home, Ida Tamsy Brooks Sheffield, (1882-1892).

**Alexander A. Scarborough** (1924-1940)

After being discharged from the Army, Alex pursued a career in research and development for the Calloway/Milliken Company and later for Kleen-tex, retiring in 1990. He is the author of *Origins of Universal Systems* and is a member of the NPA organization of international scientists. Alex and his wife, Mary, live in LaGrange, Georgia, and have three children.

**John Darby Smith, Jr. (son)** for J. D. (Jake) Smith (1913-1922)

After leaving the Home, Jake began working on a dairy farm at age 15 and was in the dairy business until his herd was sold in 1970. In 1951 Jake was named Bibb County Farmer of the Year. When his farming days were over, he became a salesman for several companies. He retired as the manager of Macon Memorial Park Cemetery. In 1980 he was named Father of the Year by the Macon Telegraph. Jake had three children, eleven grandchildren and three great-grandchildren.

**William Kirby Smith, Sr.** (1913-1922)

After William left the Home, he lived with his father.  He then joined the Army and served 30 years and retired as a Master Sergeant in 1964.  Following his retirement, he bought a farm in Bleckley County, Georgia.  He was a very successful farmer for more than ten years raising corn, cotton and soy beans.  He was named Farmer of the Year by Bleckley County.

# *Acknowledgements*

*Patches of the Quilt* would never have been possible without the help of many people. First, we want to thank the storytellers who grew up at the Home, who at Homecomings held us spellbound with their accounts of life at the Home years ago. To the authors who gave us a glimpse of their lives as children and youth we are grateful.

This book is about the love and care that children have received across the years at the Methodist Home. We want to thank Dr. Steve L. Rumford for his compassionate heart for children and for his vision that every child arriving at the Home receives the gift of a quilt. The title, example, and guiding metaphor – *Patches of the Quit* – was his gift to this endeavor. We are grateful for your unwavering encouragement for this project that has spanned eight years.

A. Louise Staman, our editor and publisher, saw the manuscript as a diamond in the rough. She brought to this work her excitement and passion for what this book could be. And her enthusiasm was contagious. Her years of experience as an award-winning writer and publisher lifted this project to a level of excellence beyond our wildest expectations. We give thanks for your kindness, patience and guidance. We will always be grateful for your belief in us and in the importance of this endeavor.

Our appreciation goes to Joann Chase who helped to edit the stories and brought the scattered materials into a coherent first draft. Without her tireless efforts this project may have stalled in its tracks. We are indebted to Judy Peterman who spent countless hours transcribing and editing the stories and toward the end of the process corresponded with the authors and prepared the manuscript to be sent to the publisher.  Finally, we want to thank Carole Chase who rose to the challenge of a daunting manuscript in its roughest form.  Her critical eye, invaluable suggestions and corrections immensely improved the quality of this book.

From the beginning we felt that photographs would be an important part of this story.  Alumni from the Home sent photographs from all over the country.  We are grateful to the following persons for lending us pictures from their childhoods: Zimmie Goings, Mary Alice Roth, Alex Scarborough, and Charles Hall.  In addition, we express our thanks to the generous permissions we obtained to use the photos and archives in the National Archives in Washington D.C. and the Middle Georgia Archives at the Washington Memorial Library in Macon, GA, both of which have added depth and a broader perspective to our book.

We also want to express our appreciation to the countless number of quilters who have lovingly stitched and given more than one thousand quilts for our children.

Finally, we would like to express our sincere appreciation to our wonderful Alumni Association.  Without their advice, encouragement and financial support, this book would not exist.

# *Afterword*

The Methodist Home for Children and Youth has a rich history and a vibrant future. For 136 years the Home has touched the lives of more than 10,000 children, restoring their childhoods and offering each child a future and a hope. However, across the years almost unnoticed a quiet force has been at work bringing healing, new life and at times – surprises.

The stock market crash of 1929 was a major threat to all agencies supported by charity. The Methodist Home was no exception. It was on the brink of bankruptcy. The possibility of closing the Home was seriously discussed in a meeting of the Board of Trustees and was recorded in the minutes.

In the depths of the Depression, when food, leather and money were not to be found – God's spirit moved in a mighty way. In 1934 a magnificent bequest of a quarter of a million dollars was received from Dr. Thomas Murdock McIntosh. He was one of the first doctors in the state to perform cataract surgery and loved children although he never married and had no children of his own. His timely gift was used to stabilize the Home financially and refurbish the dining hall and kitchen. An endowment in his name continues to bless children today and will touch the lives of children yet unborn. Dr. Tom's gift was the first of several occasions where "a surprise blessing" (as Dr. Steve Rumford calls it) was to make a huge difference in the Methodist Home and in the lives of our children.

As our country prospered in the years between 1940 and 1970, the Home flourished as well. Education was emphasized and a college degree was encouraged. The Home recognized and rewarded its high school students on honor roll. This emphasis on getting a good education had positive results. During a period in the early sixties there were three boys from the Home at Emory University, one at the University of Georgia and two girls in college – one at Georgia College and State University and the other at Hunter College in Alabama.

It was also during this period that the farm was phased out. The city of Macon, slowly moving north, finally surrounded the Home on all sides. A dairy farm in the middle of a beautiful residential area did not make for good neighbors, especially when our cows would find an opening in the fence, walk the streets and eat our neighbors' prized camellias. Working on the farm was replaced by a myriad of after-school activities, especially school sports. Several boys from the Home excelled in football, basketball and track. One of our outstanding football players went on to play defensive back for the University of South Carolina.

From the mid-eighties to the present time there has been unprecedented growth in terms of children served, facilities improved and expanded, and the development of a professionally trained staff. The Methodist Home has become a model agency accredited by The Council on Accreditation of New York and Eagle of the United Methodist Association and continues to impact the way Georgia treats her children.

Prior to 1985, there had been one new building constructed in sixty years. Since 1985, there have been seventeen buildings either built or acquired on five sites across South Georgia and over $20,000,000 in improvements. At the present time the Home serves an average of 127 children in residential care and 130 in other services for a total of 257 children served every day. In addition to the Macon campus, the Home provides care for children in Americus, Valdosta, Columbus, St. Marys and Waverly Hall. The expansion of the past 20 years did not just happen; it took place under the capable leadership of Dr. Steve L. Rumford, the President/CEO, who would be the first to attest to God's surprise blessings all along the way.

In the past few years the Methodist Home for Children and Youth has received awards on local, state and national levels. The

Home was given the "The Organization of the Year" award in 2006 at the annual convention of the United Methodist Association in Boston. In 2007 the Home received "The Organization of the Year" award from the Georgia Association of Homes and Services for Children. Also in the same year The Better Business Bureau in Macon honored the Methodist Home with the 2007 Torch Award for Ethical Practice. In June of 2008 Dr. Rumford was given the "Eugene Calhoun Lifetime Achievement Award for 2008" by the Georgia Association of Homes and Services for Children.

For decades the children of the Home longed for a gymnasium, a place to play on freezing, scorching and rainy days. In the late thirties there was even serious talk of building a gymnasium, but when the Japanese bombed Pearl Harbor in 1941, they essentially bombed the prospects of a gym. However in the early days of the Twenty–First Century, Ruth Ham Ferguson, a girl who grew up at the Home in the 1940s, gave a million dollars that became the down payment for a building complex that included her long-awaited gym. Another surprise blessing.

The Rumford Center, dedicated in 2004, includes a gymnasium, a walking track, a weight room, a racquetball court, and a beautiful dining room. On the fourth floor there is a state-of-the art conference center that hosts groups from across the state where the training and equipping of professional child care workers takes place almost every day of the week.

Professionals from across the country and from around the world visit our campus. Most recently the person responsible for all the state-owned orphanages in the Republic of Russia paid an official visit to our Macon campus to listen and ask questions. She was fascinated by the quilts she saw on display in our buildings. When she heard that all of our children receive a handmade quilt upon their arrival, she was visibly moved.

Courtesy of Walter Elliott

## Rumford Center – the Main Building of the Home Today

From the days when we served 26 children with a handful of staff until now, our mission has remained the same:

- to restore childhoods,
- to empower children with a faith that is unshakable, and
- to give children their best chance to succeed in life

In this book, you have been given a rare glimpse into the lives of the men and women who grew up on these sacred grounds. As you reflect on these stories, I would like to extend to you two invitations: First, please pray for our children and against the forces that would destroy them. Secondly, I invite you to become part of the life of the Methodist Home. Below you will find listed the ways you can weave yourself into this sacred story.

Dr. Edwin Chase
Director of the Family Institute and Special Gifts
Editor of *Patches of the Quilt,* and former resident of the Home

# AN INVITATION

*If you wish* to make a difference in the life of a child….

   *If you wish* to give a gift to the Methodist Home….

You can make your check payable to:

> The Methodist Home for Children and Youth
> P.O. Box 2525
> Macon, Georgia 31203-2525

For more ways to make a contribution to the Methodist Home, please visit our website at:www.themethodisthome.org.  To include the Methodist Home in your will, please visit us at: information@foundationmch.org

**All profits from the sale of *Patches of the Quilt* will support the ministry of the Methodist Home for Children and Youth**.